Think RE! 3

D0549675

Michael Brewer • Janet Dyson

Gary Green • Ruth Mantin • Cavan Wood

Series editor: Janet Dyson Consultant: Pamela Draycott

www.heinemann.co.uk
✓ Free online support
✓ Useful weblinks
✓ 24 hour online ordering

01865 888058

Heinemann

Inspiring generations

Heinemann Educational Publishers
Halley Court, Jordan Hill, Oxford OX2 8EJ
Part of Harcourt Education

Heinemann is the registered trademark of
Harcourt Education Limited

First published 2005

10 09 08 07 06 05
10 9 8 7 6 5 4 3 2 1

British Library Cataloguing in Publication Data is available
from the British Library on request.

10-digit ISBN: 0 435 30735 5
13-digit ISBN: 978 0 435 30735 6

Copyright notice

Produced by Bridge Creative Services Ltd

Original illustrations © Harcourt Education Limited, 2005
Illustrated by Andrew Skilleter and Jane Smith

Printed in the UK by Scotprint

Cover photo: © Bruce Coleman

Picture research by Ginny Stroud-Lewis

Acknowledgements

Thanks to the teachers and students in Barking and Dagenham and Southend on Sea for their help in trialling some of the material and their helpful feedback.
Every effort has been made to contact copyright holders of material reproduced in this book. Any omissions will be rectified in subsequent printings if notice is given to the publishers.

Faith readers

Thanks to the following for help and advice on all religious content:

Jonathan Brandman	Board of Deputies of British Jews
Rasamandala Das	Oxford Centre for Vishnu Hindu Studies
Dick Powell	Assistant Diocesan Secretary, Diocesan House
Anil Goonewardene	Buddhist Society
Nalia Salim	Stratford School
Bhupinder Singh	United Sikhs

Copyright

Photo acknowledgements

The publishers would like to thank the following for permission to use photographs:
Alamy/Andrew Holt p.97 (top); Alamy/David Crausby pp.93, 109; Alamy/Dan Atkin p.105; Alamy/Karen Robinson p.46; Alamy/Mary Evans p.9 (bottom); Alamy/Molly Cooper p.103 (centre top); Alamy/Pat Behnke p.69; Art Archive p.44; Corbis/Annie Griffiths p.83; Corbis/Barbara Davidson/Dallas Morning News p.84; Corbis/Bettmann pp.30 (both), 40; Corbis/B.S.P.I p.15; Corbis/David Kadlubowski p.66 (right); Corbis/Don Mason pp.103 (right), 104; Corbis/Hulton Deutsch p.76; Corbis/Jean-Philippe Arles/Reuters p.13 top; Corbis/Kimbell Art Museum pp.5, 19; Corbis/Mario Beauregard p.48 (left); Corbis/Mark Jenkinson p.70; Corbis/Michael St.Maur Sheil p.103 (left); Corbis/Murdo Macleod p.43; Corbis/Reuters pp.71, 75, 89, 91; Corbis/Robert Holmes p.59; Corbis/Sanford/Agliolo p.32 (middle); Corbis/Streetstock Images p.62; Corbis/Sygma pp.7, 68; Corrymeela society p.77; Digital Vision p.32 (left); Getty Images/Melanie Acevedo p.96; Getty Images/Stephen Marks p.58; Granada TV pp.10, 63; Harcourt Index pp.21, 37; John Christopher Wright/Leeds postcards p.107 (left); Julia Bolton Holloway p.97 (bottom); Luke Warm/Leeds Postcards p.99; Mary Evans Picture Library p.52 (bottom); M.C.Escher's "Convex and Concave" ©2005 The M.C.Escher Company-Holland. All rights reserved.www.mcescher.com p.6; Photofusion/Brenda Prince pp.79, 80 (bottom); Photofusion/Molly Cooper p.85; Photofusion/Paul Baldesare p.64; Photofusion/Paula Solloway p.86; Rex Features/A.Macdonald p.107 (right); Rex features/CPL Archive/Everett p.53; Rex features/David White p.80 (top); Rex Features/Geoff Robinson p.48 (right); Rex Features/Mark Brewer p.103 (bottom centre); Rex Features/Roger-Voillet p.28 (top); Rex Features/Sipa press p.66 (left); Rex Features/SNAP p.52 (top); Robert Harding Library p.27; Robert Spence/Society of the Religious Society of Friends p.78; Science Photo Library/Doug Allan p.28 (bottom); Science Photo Library/James King-Holmes p.45; Science Photo Library/Steve Allen p.60; Science Photo Library/Will & Deni McIntyre p.51; Science & Society Picture Library p.22; Still Pictures pp.57, 73; Tate London p.101; The Art Archive/British Library p.25; The Bridgeman Art Library/Musee des Beaux-Arts p.35; Topfoto p.17; Topfoto/AP p.42; Topfoto/DPA/SSK/The Image Works p.9 top; Topfoto/Fortean p.47; Topfoto/Lucas Films Ltd. P.16; Topfoto/PA p.13 (bottom); World Religions/Christine Osborne pp.65, 82; Zefa/G.Baden p.32 (right).

CONTENTS

1 WHAT IS TRUTH?

THE BIGGER PICTURE

In this chapter you will analyse the importance that religious and non-religious people attach to the idea of truth. You will explore some of the problems that people have when they claim to know the 'truth' about something.

WHAT?

You will:

- reflect on what 'truth' might be
- suggest ways in which people decide what is true
- evaluate whether stories can convey the truth about what it means to be human
- investigate ideas about revelation.

HOW?

By:

- studying truth claims in Christianity, Islam, Judaism and Buddhism
- examining the role of stories in religion
- interpreting different religious approaches to truth
- exploring how post-modern ideas influence people's understanding of truth
- understanding the importance of revelation to religious believers.

WHY?

Because:

- truth is important when making claims about the world
- many religious believers might claim to know the truth as found in their religion
- to understand religion you need to have a good knowledge of the ideas of revelation, and insight into ways in which people seek the truth.

KEY IDEAS

- Religious believers hold different beliefs about truth that affect how they live.
- There are different methods of exploring truth, for example, through religion, science, literature and art.
- Stories can reveal the truth even though they might not be historically accurate.
- Some religious people gain insight into truth by revelation, conversion and meditation.
- Zen Buddhists believe that truth is revealed in a moment of insight rather than through meditation.
- Post-modern philosophers have tried to settle the question of whether we can ever find 'the truth'.

KEY WORDS

Conscience	Culture
Turin Shroud	Parable
Revelation	Divine Revelation
General Revelation	Special Revelation
Reversion	Conversion
Zen Buddhism	Nirvana
Enlightenment	Koan
Haiku	Meditation
Modernism	Post-modernism
Metanarrative	

Zen Buddhism inspires many works of art.

In this lesson you will:
- investigate what is meant by 'truth'
- explore how people decide whether something is true
- draw your own conclusions about truth.

WHAT IS TRUTH?

The Bible (John 18: 38) describes how, when Jesus was on trial, the Roman Governor Pilate asked him 'What is truth?' Pilate did not wait for an answer. For centuries, people have been trying to work out the answer to this question.

The Oxford dictionary definition of truth is 'the quality or state of being truthful'. But how do we know the difference between something that is true and something that is untrue?

HOW DO PEOPLE LOOK FOR TRUTH?

People have looked to both religion and science to help them find the truth.

- Religion is one way in which many people look for truth. It can help them to answer ultimate questions such as 'Who am I?' and 'Why am I here?'
- People have also used science to help them answer such questions. Scientists believe that the truth should be 'proven' through experiment and observation.
- Where else do you think people might look for and 'find' truth?

THINK ABOUT IT!

1. a) Make a list of six questions about life which you think are important.
   b) Share your questions with a friend. Choose two questions and explain why you think they are important.

IS TRUTH SIMPLE OR COMPLICATED?

One question that both religion and science continue to try to answer is 'Is the truth simple or complicated?'

The idea that truth is simple is called reductionism. This idea was developed in the Middle Ages by a thinker called William of Ockham (c.1288–1348). He suggested that to reach the truth, you need to get to the simplest possible explanation of an event or idea. For example, you could argue that human history reflects a struggle between the rich and the poor. But can the truth be that simple? For example, how do you account for the influence of inventors and artists on human history?

Perhaps events are like a rainbow made up of many different colours: we need to look at several different reasons all coming together as to why things are as they are.

Truth can be very complicated. Which part of this painting is true? Is it all true?

● WHAT IS YOUR IDEA OF TRUTH?

Your idea of truth will be influenced by the world around you and your experiences within it, such as:

● your education
● your friends and family
● your religious or non-religious beliefs
● the media.

Your sense of truth will also help you to understand the world around you.

🎧 **The media can have a great influence over what we believe to be true. In the film *The Truman Show*, a television company constructs a reality for one man to live in. He believes that the world he experiences is real and that what he is told about it is the truth.**

● FIVE WAYS OF FINDING TRUTH

There are several ways in which we come to know the world around us, for example:

[1] Conscience: Your sense of right and wrong will influence what you believe about yourself and others. This might be an 'inner voice' that tells you whether your actions are right or wrong. For example, have you ever said something to a friend and then realised that you have been rude to him or her? Some people think that the 'inner voice' might be God.

[2] *Reason.* Your ability to think logically has a huge influence on what you believe to be true. In mathematics and science, people try to find patterns of numbers or events in order to better understand the world around them. Have you ever carried out a scientific experiment and accepted the results as being true? Many people think that God has given 'minds' for humans to use.

[3] *Authority.* You might believe that it is important to listen to another person who you respect or to follow religious teachings to find the truth. Some religious believers listen to the authority of a religious leader like the Pope, or refer to the authority of religious scriptures, for example, the Guru Granth Sahib or the Qur'an. In science, someone who is a Professor or who has received an award has authority.

Five ways of finding truth

[4] *Feelings.* If you have strong feelings about a person, idea or situation, then these feelings might influence how you understand the truth. We use our emotions to help us judge, or make up our minds about, the world around us.

[5] *Peer group.* You might come to think that something is true because many people of your own age believe that it is. For example, have you ever judged a person based on something that a friend has told you, without really knowing that person for yourself?

[6] Culture. The traditions, religions and other beliefs of the people around you will influence the way you think about the world. For example, a person living in the UK is likely to have different experiences and beliefs than somone in Africa.

THINK ABOUT IT!

2. Which of the six ways of finding truth listed above do you trust most? Why? Give reasons for your answers.

3. Which of the six ways of finding truth listed above do you trust least? Why? Give reasons for your answers.

In this lesson you will:
- explore how history helps people to find the truth
- analyse religious ideas about history and truth in Christianity and Buddhism
- express your own ideas about whether religious stories can be true.

KEY WORDS

Turin Shroud a piece of cloth that Jesus' body was supposed to have been wrapped in after the crucifixion

THINK ABOUT IT!

1. Working in pairs, make a list of the ways in which a detective might go about solving a crime. Represent your ideas using a pictogram.

WHAT REALLY HAPPENED?

A good detective collects evidence from different places and then works out what the evidence means. By using the clues from the evidence, the detective might be able to conclude what happened, who did it and why. However, not all the evidence might agree on the same solution; for example, witnesses might say very different things.

Historians also try to find out what is true. The evidence they use might include documents such as letters, birth certificates or newspaper articles, or artefacts such as pots and jewellery. However, historians must bear in mind that:
- historical evidence can be viewed in different ways
- some of the items might be biased; they may only tell one side of a story.

Historians might agree that an event happened, but they might be divided as to why it happened and how significant it was.

Below is some of the historical evidence that two religions – Christianity and Buddhism – use to support their beliefs.

THINK ABOUT IT!

2. What problems might a religious person face when using historical evidence to support their faith?

What evidence do we have for the existence of Jesus?

People have debated over many years whether Jesus existed and if so who he was. The main historical evidence given for his existence includes:
- The New Testament, especially the Four Gospels: for Christians these provide strong evidence of who Jesus was and what he did. However...

The first account was not written down until about 65 CE.

The books were written for different purposes at different times. For example, some books were written to show that Jesus was the Son of God and to convince others of that.

Artefacts such as the **Turin Shroud** are used as physical evidence that Jesus lived.

- Historians of the time, such as the Jewish writer Josephus and the Roman writer Pliny, both wrote about Jesus and agree with many of the details of the Gospels, even though both of them were against Christianity.
- Archaeologists have found inscriptions on tombs showing that people believed in Jesus just a few years after he is said to have been alive. For example, a gravestone was found in Jerusalem which was dated 70 CE and refers to a person going to be with Jesus after they had died.

There is scientific evidence to suggest that the Turin Shroud is a fake that was created long after the time of Jesus.

However, even if you accept that there is enough evidence to believe that Jesus existed you might not think there is enough evidence to prove he was the 'Son of God'.

Evidence in Buddhism

For many centuries there was debate outside the Buddhist community as to whether the Buddha existed as a historical character. Scholars now believe there is some historical and archaeological evidence for the existence of Siddhartha Gautama, the man who became known as the Buddha. For example, written evidence of the Buddha's existence is found:

● on the pillar of Ashoka near Bodh Gaya in India
● in the texts of non-Buddhist writers.

Although the stories of the Buddha's experiences cannot be investigated by historians, some Buddhists use stories about the Buddha as evidence that certain events took place.

The Four Sights

When he was still a Prince, Siddhartha Gautama visited the city four times. He saw four different types of people: an old man, an ill man, a dead man and a holy man.

● Some Buddhists think that this actually happened.
● Others think that it could have been a vision.
● Others simply believe that it was a story told after the time of the Buddha, to explain his teaching.

Whilst Buddhists are united by the belief that the Buddha existed, for many Buddhists it isn't important whether everything the Buddha said and did happened exactly as it is recorded. Many Buddhists believe that it is the meaning of the Buddha's life that matters the most. They believe these events to be true in the sense that they reveal truths about the way we should live.

? THINK ABOUT IT!

3. Is it important that the events on which religions are based really happened?
   ● What might a Christian think?
   ● What do you think?

   Give reasons for your answer, showing that you have thought about it from more than one point of view.

4. **a)** Write down at least three questions you would like to ask about the story of the Four Sights.
   b) As a class, vote on which question you would like to discuss.

5. What might a Buddhist say about the importance of his or her faith being historically true? Give reasons for your answer.

🎧 **How do people know what the Buddha and Jesus looked like? Does every artist interpret the image in his or her own way? If so, can there be any truth in these images?**

In this lesson you will:
- analyse the importance of religious and non-religious stories for explaining truths
- investigate the importance of parables for Christians
- explore how stories can provide information and ideas about the world
- express your own views on issues raised by stories.

KEY WORDS

Parable a story told to illustrate a religious or moral idea

HOW CAN A STORY BE TRUE IF IT NEVER HAPPENED?

Jack Priestley was a senior lecturer in the study of Religious Education at the University of Exeter. He loved to tell stories to make his points clear.

When Jack Priestley was a lecturer in a Zambian Teacher Training College, a student told his class the following story.

THINK ABOUT IT!

1. What do you think this story means? Discuss your ideas with a partner.

There was once a hungry hyena searching for food who arrived at a fork in the path. Either side there were large amounts of food. The hyena hesitated about whether to go to the left or the right? It could not decide and tried to go in both directions at the same time. It ripped its body apart.

Half of the group believed this story to be true. The others did not and asked where and when did this happen? In the end the class concluded that, 'This story is true not because it happened but because it shows that greed destroys the greedy.'

Soap operas – are they true to life?

THINK ABOUT IT!

2. Do you think this story is successful in showing how greed can destroy people? Give reasons for your answers.

Think about a soap opera or TV drama that you have watched recently. The story was probably fiction, but did any of the characters or situations in it reflect your's or others' experiences of real life?

'Story making is our medium for coming to terms with the surprises and oddities of the human condition.'

Jerome Bruner, Psychologist

Today, stories like the hyena story opposite can seem a little strange. Yet they are like a code. If you understand a little about the time and place in which they were written, or about the people who first told them, then it is easier to crack the code and understand their relevance.

JESUS AND PARABLES

A **parable** is a story that many religious teachers use to teach something important. Jesus often used parables to put his points across. These stories were about things or events that were familiar to his audience, to help them understand difficult ideas about God or morality. Jesus told parables in a way that made them easy to listen to and memorable.

However, it was not always immediately obvious to people what the point of the parable was. The Gospel writers think that this was deliberate, because Jesus wanted people to go away and think about the stories.

Two of the parable stories Jesus told are below:

The mustard seed

'The Kingdom of Heaven is like a mustard seed which a man took and planted in a field. Though it is the smallest of all your seeds, yet when it grows, it is the largest of garden plants and becomes a tree, so that the birds of the air come and perch in the branches.'

Matthew 13: 31–2

The lost coin

'Suppose a woman has ten silver coins and loses one. Does she not light a lamp, sweep the house and search carefully until she finds it? And when she finds it, she calls her friends and neighbours together and says "Rejoice with me; I have found my lost coin." In the same way, I tell you, there is rejoicing in the presence of the angels of God over one sinner who repents.'

Luke 15: 8–10

THINK ABOUT IT!

3. Jesus said that the meaning of his parables would be clear to 'those who had eyes to see and ears to hear'. What do you think he might have meant by this?

4. Read through the two parables above.
   a) What point do you think Jesus was trying to put across by these stories?
   b) How might Jesus tell these stories today, so that they are accessible to a modern audience?

In this lesson you will:
- reflect on your own experiences of realising that you have understood something
- explore the concept of Divine Revelation by reading accounts of people's experiences.

Some people would say that this experience of sudden realisation and understanding is a **revelation**.

- **Divine revelation** is the term used by religious people to describe how they come to know the truth about God or the deities they believe in.

- Some people think that God can be seen in creation or the natural world. They call this idea **general revelation**, as it is available for all to see.

'God made us and we should wonder at it.'

Spanish proverb.

- **Special revelation** is the belief that God is revealed in particular ways to people. For many Christians, the idea that God became a human being as Jesus is the most important moment of revelation. Many Christians believe that in his life, death and resurrection, Jesus revealed the character of God.

DO PEOPLE EXPERIENCE DIVINE REVELATION IN DIFFERENT WAYS?

Divine Revelation can occur in a variety of ways, as shown in the diagram below.

THINK ABOUT IT!

1. In pairs, share an experience of suddenly realising and understanding something that you had been taught at school. How did this understanding happen?

2. Could any of these claims to revelation convince you? Give reasons for your answer.

3. How do you think a person who goes to Lourdes and does not get healed might feel?

Conscience – some people believe that the sense of right and wrong is a gift from God

Holy books – for example, Muslims believe the Qur'an was revealed by Allah to Muhammad

Divine Revelation can occur through...

Miracles – some Christians claim to have experienced a personal encounter with God or a significant religious figure, such as the Virgin Mary

Prayer – for example, when people claim that their personal prayers have been answered

Experiences of key members of the religion – for example, Sikhs believe that Guru Nanak was taken up to heaven for three days and had a special experience of God

St Bernadette (1844–1879) was a young girl when she claimed to have met the Virgin Mary in the town of Lourdes in France. Today, many people claim to have experienced a miraculous healing after visiting Lourdes. However, others go there and are not healed.

A bully becomes a Christian

The book of Acts in the New Testament tells the story of Saul's conversion. When Saul was travelling from the city of Damascus in Syria to arrest Christians, he was blinded by a light and fell from his horse. A voice spoke to him and when Saul asked who the voice belonged to, it replied, 'I am Jesus, whom you persecute.'

Saul eventually regained his sight and decided that he would become a follower of Christ. He changed his name to Paul, to show that he had changed.

A pop star's experience

In the 1970s, the musician Cat Stevens was on holiday in the USA. He went swimming and suddenly found himself in difficulty. Terrified that he would drown, he promised that he would commit himself to God if he was rescued. He found himself on the shore, safe. He decided to become a Muslim and changed his name to Yusuf Islam. Since Muslims believe that all people were originally Muslim believers, Yusuf is considered a **revert** rather than a **convert**.

C.S. Lewis finds God

In 1929, the writer C.S. Lewis was convinced there was no God. He was a good friend of J.R.R. Tolkien, who wrote *The Lord of the Rings*. One evening, they went for a walk around the grounds of the Oxford college they worked in. Lewis listened to Tolkien's arguments about the existence of God. When he returned to his room, Lewis decided to kneel down and pray. He says in his autobiography that he 'earnestly desired not to meet God' but that he eventually gave in and admitted God's presence.

? THINK ABOUT IT!

4. Read through the three experiences described above, then consider the following questions.
   a) Why was the experience so significant to the person involved?
   b) Does the account have meaning for anyone else?
   c) Does each account prove anything?

5. Do you find some forms of revelation more difficult to believe in than others? Give reasons for your answers.

6. Would any of these experiences of revelation convince you that there is a God?

In this lesson you will:
- understand the key ideas of Zen Buddhism
- explore ways in which Zen Buddhists might look for truth
- interpret different forms of spiritual expression in Zen Buddhism.

KEY WORDS

Zen Buddhism a tradition of Buddhism from the school of Mahayana Buddhism, developed in China and Japan

Meditation calming and strengthening the mind by concentrating

Nirvana state of being free from confusion, greed or hatred

Enlightenment the process of becoming aware of the truth of existence which frees a person to obtain Nirvana

Koan paradoxical questions used by some Zen Buddhists to discover truth

Haiku a type of poem devised by Zen Buddhists

WHAT IS THE WAY OF ZEN?

Buddhism is a religion that does not believe in a creator God, so the issue of truth is never linked to the debate about God's revelation.

Zen is a tradition of Buddhism that encourages its followers to think in new ways in order to find the truth. It encourages people to look beyond what they see and to **meditate** in order to achieve **Nirvana** and **Enlightenment**.

HOW DO ZEN BUDDHISTS LOOK FOR TRUTH?

Koans

One way in which Zen Buddhism encourages new thinking is by the use of **koans**. A koan is a saying that might startle or confuse people. Koans are often questions that make a person think deeply. Two famous koans are: 1. Does the man look at the mountain or the mountain look at the man?

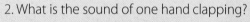

2. What is the sound of one hand clapping?

THINK ABOUT IT!

1. Do you think that a belief in God makes it easier or harder to believe in truth? Give reasons for your answer.

THINK ABOUT IT!

2. **a)** What do you think these koans might mean to Buddhists?
   b) Why might Buddhists think these koans are important?

There are not supposed to be rational, sensible answers to these koans. Instead, they are designed to test the enlightenment of Buddhists. Koans help people to see the limitations in their thinking and understanding of the world.

Zen masters

Although Zen Buddhism encourages people to listen to the wise teachings of Zen masters or the Buddha, it also warns that truth cannot be found simply by listening to other people. One Zen saying is 'If you see a Buddha on the road, kill him'. This is not encouraging Zen Buddhists to commit murder but to find the truth for themselves.

Haikus

Zen Buddhists also reflect on the nature of reality through a type of poem called a **haiku**. These poems are intended to reveal the truth of the world in a few syllables. A Zen Buddhist called Basho Matsuo (1644–94) developed this form of poetry.

'Still pond
A frog jumps in
Kerplunk!'

A haiku poem by Basho Matsuo.

◖ **Zen gardens celebrate the idea of simplicity**

Zen gardens

Some Zen Buddhists make sand gardens. This is because the simple designs of the gardens, which represent the world in miniature, help them to meditate and see reality in perpsective.

Martial arts

Other Zen Buddhists use martial arts such as judo, karate and Kung-Fu to train their bodies and as a form of moving meditation. They believe there is a connection between being physically fit and understanding the world in a new way, and that martial arts can therefore help the mind move beyond the material world towards Enlightenment.

THINK ABOUT IT!

3. How might being physically fit help you to see the world in a new way? Give reasons for your answers.

Zen, like all other forms of Buddhism, teaches that a person's understanding of what is real is marred by the fact that he or she is full of greed, anger and ignorance. The Buddha called these states of mind the 'three poisons'. Buddhists believe that it is only when we understand and are free of these poisons that we can reach *satori* or Enlightenment. Finding simple explanations of truth is one way in which Zen Buddhists try to better understand their mental states and reach Enlightenment.

THINK ABOUT IT!

4. For each of the aspects of Zen Buddhism on these pages, think about the following questions.
   a) How might greed, anger and ignorance stop you from finding the truth?
   b) Is truth simple or complex?
   c) How can you be sure you have found truth?

5. Write a haiku of three lines about searching for the truth.

In this lesson you will:
- reflect on how philosophers have tried to answer the question 'What is truth?'
- analyse the effect of post-modern ideas on society
- explore the impact of post-modern ideas on religion.

KEY WORDS

Modernism a philosophy based on reason and science

Post-modernism a group of ideas that question whether there is objective truth

Metanarrative a 'big story' such as a religion or a political belief that helps shape a person's life

It can often be difficult to work out what is true in a world dominated by the media. How can we be sure that what we see or read is the truth? Is everything we see on the television true? For example, even a programme like the news is carefully edited. Some news stories are rejected whilst others are included.

WHAT IS MODERNISM?

Modernism is a philosophical belief that started in the late-nineteenth century. It claims truth can be found by:
- using science and scientific ways of thinking
- being objective, not relying on feelings or emotions
- finding rational explanations for everything, even for the supernatural.

POST-MODERNISM – IS TRUTH WHAT YOU MAKE IT?

In the second half of the twentieth century, philosophers began to talk about **post-modernism**. Post-modernism is a theory that states that because things are always changing there can be no absolute truths. Everything is shaped by a particular time, place or community. You cannot use one belief, be it religious, political or scientific, to understand the way the world works, because all beliefs are limited.

THINK ABOUT IT!

3. Think about the statement 'Ghosts do not exist'.
   a) How would a modernist respond to this?
   b) How would a post-modernist respond?

THINK ABOUT IT!

1. Look at the three bullet points about modernism.
   a) Which do you agree with?
   b) Which don't you agree with? Give reasons for your answers.

2. Does modernism pose a threat to religion? Take each bullet point in turn and write down one reason why that belief might challenge religion.

HOW DO POST-MODERNISTS MAKE SENSE OF THE WORLD?

Post-modernists argue that **metanarratives** (big stories) help people to order their lives and find meaning when previously they may have been confused. Post-modernists are suspicious of metanarratives and believe they are used by people in power to decide what is 'true'. These 'big stories' include religious and political beliefs. Some political beliefs provide people with a world view that dominates all they see – for example, a Marxist believes that issues of class, money and power shape the world.

Movie makers often use the idea of the metanarrative to build their stories. The *Star Wars* series of films creates an alternative society and history, and imagines its own religion based on the supernatural power of 'The Force'.

● HOW HAS POST-MODERNISM AFFECTED RELIGION?

Religions are metanarratives: they provide their followers with a comprehensive view of reality.

● For Christians, history reveals a creator, God, who has acted through the life, death and resurrection of Jesus Christ. The story of Jesus provides Christians with hope and calls on them to challenge the way they live now.

● For Buddhists, the life and teaching of the Buddha can help them to better understand the nature of reality. The story of the Buddha also offers the possibility of Enlightenment.

Post-modernism makes people aware of these many competing 'big stories' and argues that there are many different ways of looking at the same idea. It also highlights the importance of putting your particular message across in way that best communicates with people today. For example, some Christians have developed 'alternative worship', which combines religious rituals and practices from the past with modern methods, such as video and music.

● HINDUISM AND POST-MODERNISM

Hinduism supplies not just one but many metanarratives. It has been said that every village in India and every Hindu community across the world has a different Hinduism. For many people, Hinduism should therefore be seen as a family of religions that have many things in common.

Stories of deities and special human beings are important to Hindus because they are ways of communicating complex religious ideas. One of these stories, the *Mahabharata*, tells of how Krishnan – a key Hindu deity – acted as a charioteer to Prince Arjuna at the Battle of Kurukshetra. From the conversation between Krishna and Arjuna, many important Hindu ideas were developed, such as destiny, karma and moksha.

Hindus also use another set of stories called *The Ramayana*. The theme of these stories is duty or dharma. They focus on Rama (one of the forms of the god Vishnu) who, with his wife Sita and others, seeks to defeat evil, symbolised by the demon Ravana.

🎧 **Rama faced the demon Ravana in his quest to defeat evil.**

THINK ABOUT IT!

4. In your own words explain what a metanarrative is.

5. Many metanarratives are about the struggle between good and evil. Why do you think this is?

WHAT THE TASK IS ALL ABOUT:

You have been asked to direct a major film about the life of Jesus. You know from your work in RE that, for Christians, the most important part of the story is the death and resurrection of Jesus. Your problem is how to show the resurrection story in your film when there are several different accounts of what happened.

WHAT YOU NEED TO DO TO COMPLETE THE TASK:

a) Start by comparing the different accounts in Mark and Luke's gospels and make a list of the similarities and differences. You may also want to look at the accounts of this event in the gospels of Matthew and John.

b) Decide what the key idea about the resurrection is that you must get across in the film and summarize it in one sentence.

c) Use a story board to plan the scenes and dialogue for your film; try to include ways of using symbolizm to show the beliefs which underlie the story.

d) Write a press release for the film explaining how you have made your decisions about the resurrection scene and what 'truth' you think the film will show.

EXTENSION QUESTIONS

● How do you think Christians will react to your film?
● Explain whether or not you think it matters that there are differences in the versions of the resurrection story.

TO ACHIEVE	YOU WILL NEED TO
Level 4	Show that you understand the importance of the resurrection for Christians and that there might be different ways of interpreting the Gospel accounts of what happened. Reflect on your own response to the story and what is meant by 'truth'.
Level 5	Use your understanding of Christianity and your imagination to show the meaning of the resurrection for Christians, including the use of symbolism. Pose some questions about the meaning of 'truth'.
Level 6	Show that you have thought about different ways of expressing religious beliefs. Analyse the different accounts to draw out the key beliefs. Explain why there are different ways of understanding truth.
Level 7	Critically analyze the different accounts and suggest reasons for the similarities and differences. Ask some critical questions about religions and other claims to the truth and explain your ideas clearly.

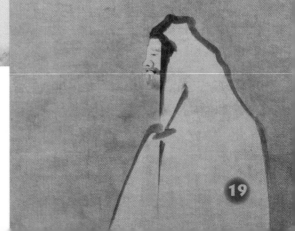

SCIENCE – HOW DID WE GET HERE?

THE BIGGER PICTURE

In this chapter you will examine some of the key scientific ideas about how the universe and human beings came to exist. You will also explore religious ideas about these origins and reasons for existence. Finally, you will think about how the universe might end.

WHAT?

You will:

- explore the relationships between science and religion and the differing questions they ask
- reflect on the implications of the Big Bang and evolution for religion
- analyse the importance of creation stories
- reflect on how the universe might end.

HOW?

By:

- evaluating theories about the Big Bang and evolution
- identifying similarities and differences between religious beliefs and scientific theories about how the world began
- investigating the life of Darwin and the Scopes Trial
- comparing scientific and religious views about the end of the world.

WHY?

Because:

- it is important to realize how religion and science shape the way you look at the world
- in order to understand theories of the Big Bang and evolution, you need to look closely at whether religion and science agree or disagree.

How did the universe begin?
How will the universe end?

KEY IDEAS

- There are two main viewpoints about how the world and the universe were created:
  1) the religious argument (the creation stories)
  2) scientific theories (for example, the Big Bang and evolution).
- Religious people have different views about the origins of the universe and these affect how religious believers live.
- The debate between religion and science often provokes very passionate discussion.
- Religion and science have contrasting and complementary views about how the world began and how it might end.

KEY WORDS

Creation	Design
Argument from design	Big Bang
Evolution	Nihilism
Trimurti	Karma
Genetic	Natural selection
Intelligent design	Creation Science
Big Crunch	Second Coming
The Rapture	

In this lesson you will:
- evaluate arguments for and against the idea that the universe was designed
- investigate the theory of the Big Bang
- express your own opinions about how the universe began.

When the spaceship Apollo 10 circled the moon in 1969, the crew were so moved by what they saw that one of them began to recite the **creation** story from the Bible.

'In the beginning, God created the heavens and the Earth.'

The Bible, Genesis 1: 1

The crew of Apollo were awestruck by the view of the moon, the stars and the Earth, and felt the words of Genesis best expressed this. They thought that there must be some sort of creator or **design** behind what they saw.

GOD AS A DESIGNER

For many religious people, the beauty of the universe and the Earth is not possible without a god. They argue that the universe is so amazing it cannot have been created by chance. This is referred to as the **argument from design**.

THINK ABOUT IT!

1. Imagine you have to create a new universe.
   - What would you keep the same?
   - What would you do differently?
   - How could you ensure exactly the right balance so that life developed?

Newton's thumb

The scientist Isaac Newton (1643–1727) believed that God designed the universe and said that the human thumb was enough to convince him of this. Every human thumb is unique, a sign to Newton that a designer God made each human being different. Newton argued that God chose to do this to show his love and individual care of the things he made. He said that what is true about a human thumb is even truer of the universe itself.

Paley's watch

For the Christian writer William Paley (1743–1805), the mystery and complexity of the universe shows that there is a designer God. Imagine, he said, you are out walking and come across a watch on the ground. You would not think that it just happened to appear there, would you? You would think that it must have been made and designed by someone. If you can believe this about a watch, why not believe there is a God who designed the universe?

The complex workings of a watch suggest that it has a designer.

● WHAT WAS THE BIG BANG?

The **Big Bang** is an event that some people believe was the beginning of the universe. They argue that the universe began when matter much smaller than the size of the eye of a needle came into existence and rapidly exploded, leading to the formation of elements such as hydrogen and helium. The Big Bang also resulted in the beginnings of gravity, which enabled some of the matter to gather into stars. Inside these stars, new compounds and gases began to develop. When these stars exploded, these vital elements were sent out into the universe, and some of them collected to form planets or stars like the Sun.

BIG PLAN OR BIG BANG?

For some people, God was involved in both the Big Bang and the development of life. Other people believe that scientific theories of the origins of the universe make it unnecessary to believe in a creator God – they believe that the universe came into existence without anyone or anything causing it.

In 1986, the scientist Richard Dawkins wrote a book about **evolution** called *The Blind Watchmaker*. He wanted to show that Paley's idea about the watch was wrong.

Dawkins argues that there is no design to the universe but that the different plants and animals are the result of evolution. Evolution is not planned, so if the world appears to be designed then this is simply an accident of evolution. Dawkins likens this accident to a blind person being able to put a watch together without knowing the instructions! A blind person might end up with a complex watch – this would not be as a result of their planning or working to a design; they just got lucky.

THINK ABOUT IT!

2. How difficult is it to imagine things coming into existence from nothing?

3. **a)** In pairs, list the arguments for the point of view that the universe is designed.
   b) Now list the arguments *against* the universe being designed.
   c) Join with another pair and share your ideas.
   d) Based on these ideas, which point of view do you agree with?

4. What would be the effect of believing that the universe was created by chance rather than designed by God? Give reasons for your answer.

Do the complex workings of the universe prove that God designed it?

2.2 WHAT DO HINDUS BELIEVE ABOUT CREATION?

In this lesson you will:
- explore key beliefs that are contained within one of the Hindu creation stories
- ask questions and suggest meanings about this Hindu creation story.

KEY WORDS

Nihilism the belief that existence has no point

Trimurti the three gods Brahma (creator), Vishnu (sustainer) and Shiva (destroyer)

Karma a teaching which states that all actions have consequences and will influence future lives

Since the beginning of humanity, people have tried to work out whether there is an ultimate meaning to life on Earth. Some people have said that there is no purpose to life and that we should learn to come to terms with that fact. This point of view is known as **nihilism**.

> 'Human life is nasty, brutish and short.'
>
> *The philosopher Thomas Hobbes (1588–1679)*

Most religious people would disagree with nihilism. For them, creation stories provide an opportunity to think about why we are here and how we should act. Such stories can also reveal why the harsher aspects of life, such as death, suffering and evil, exist.

WHAT DO HINDUS BELIEVE?

Hindus explain the cycle of life and death as being one of constant change. This cycle is reflected in the movement of souls from one body to another and in the way in which the universe is formed.

Hindus believe that there is one ultimate God or spirit called Brahman, behind everything that exists. Brahman is beyond human understanding and chooses to reveal itself by three faces, known in Hinduism as the **Trimurti**. The Trimurti is made up of:
- Brahma the Creator
- Vishnu the Sustainer
- Shiva the Destroyer.

Brahma created the world which Vishnu sustains. Shiva will destroy things as necessary. There is a natural cycle of birth, development and then death, which must continually be renewed.

This understanding has an effect on the way Hindus believe they should live. They believe that all life is full of moments of life, death and continuing existence, and that people need to understand that actions have consequences.

🎧 **Hindus believe that there is a constant cycle of life and death.**

● HOW DOES CREATION HAPPEN?

When a universe is destroyed by Shiva, nothing is left but a vast ocean. Vishnu floats on the ocean on the great snake Ananta and the universe begins again. Some Hindus say that from Vishnu's navel comes a lotus flower, which is made by the creator Brahma.

Brahma is believed by some Hindus to grow very lonely and then he desires to create again, so he splits himself into two, a male and a female. He then becomes one again and in this way all the animals, insects and living things on Earth are made. At the end of this universe, after Shiva destroys it, it is said that everything will return to the body of Vishna.

🎧 **Vishnu on the giant snake Ananta on the oceans at the beginning of a universe.**

THINK ABOUT IT!

1. In what ways are you a creator, a sustainer and a destroyer of the things around you?

● HOW LONG DOES A UNIVERSE LAST?

Hindus believe that one day for Brahma is equivalent to four thousand million years. When Brahma sleeps, the universe dies, and when he awakes, the cycle of creation begins again. In this way the cycle of life will go on forever.

> The stories of how the Trimurti make, destroy and re-make the universe remind me that there are always going to be changes going on in my life, that many universes of possibility will open and close in my life.

Maya

THINK ABOUT IT!

2. What questions would you like to ask about the Hindu creation story? Write down three questions, then share them with a partner. Choose one and outline some key points about it. Share your ideas with the class.

3. Can human beings have any control over the cycle of life, development and death? How? Are there limits to what we can do?

4. Do you think the idea of **karma** – that people reap the effects of their actions from their previous existences – is fair? Give reasons for your opinion, showing that you have thought about it from at least two different points of view.

In this lesson you will:
● explore the importance of creation stories for the Sanema tribe
● reflect on the fact that not all religions have creation stories
● compare and contrast ideas about the origins of the universe from two religions.

For some religious people, creation stories are a way of explaining the meaning of life and answering difficult questions about the way the world works. They help us to understand why the universe exists and how human beings might understand their own mysterious existence.

● Was human life planned by an intelligent being like a God?
● If existence was planned, why is there suffering in the universe?

Creation stories are often told to try to find the answers to these questions, but sometimes they only give rise to more questions!

A CREATION TALE FROM THE AMAZON

In the Amazon rainforests in South America live a tribe called the Sanema. They believe in the importance of storytelling as a way to communicate important ideas. They have survived in the forest for many generations as hunter-gatherers, but as modern industry exploits the rainforest, the Sanema's way of life is under threat.

The Curare woman hides the two tadpoles in a pot.

The Sanema creation story tells of a being called the Curare Woman and the Original Jaguar. The Jaguar enjoyed eating meat and caught the frog called Waipilli. The Jaguar made the Curare Woman cut up the frog and they ate it.

What the Jaguar did not know was that the woman saved two tadpoles called Omao and Soawe, whom she hid in a pot. The tadpoles grew rapidly and the woman hid them from Jaguar.

One day, after Jaguar had died, Omao was hungry. He went looking for Lalagi-gi, the cosmic anaconda who could show him how to grow plants. Omao was scared of Lalagi-gi, but the snake helped him to grow his plants.

Next, Omao decided to create humans. He wanted to make them out of hardwood but he found it difficult to find any hardwood trees. His brother Soawe was too lazy to find him hardwood and brought him softwood, which made Omao angry.

Omao had wanted to make humans of hardwood so that they could shed their skins when they got old and then grow a new one. The softwood would mean that they would be weak and would not live forever. He later made the snake out of some hardwood bark he found.

But Omao was angry and he left the world. In the long night, animals, insects and the ancestors of the Sanema came into existence. Still the night went on, and the currasow bird sang. When one of the ancestors shot the bird, dawn broke and, from its feathers, all the birds of the forest appeared.

All creation stories contain important truths for believers about how they should live their lives. The Sanema's creation story shows the importance of the forest to their way of life. The Sanema try to live in harmony with the natural world, seeing the forest as a living thing to be treated with respect and care; they realize that there are many dangers to life there.

THINK ABOUT IT!

1. What similarities can you find between the Sanema creation story and the Hindu creation story on pages 24–5? What differences are there?

2. 'The Sanema creation story is so strange that it cannot teach us anything.' Do you agree with this statement? Give reasons for your answer, showing that you have thought about it from more than one point of view.

3. The Sanema try to live in harmony with nature. How might people who don't live in the rainforest try to live in harmony with nature?

● WHAT MIGHT A BUDDHIST SAY?

Some religions do not have a creation story. For Buddhists, the question of how or why the universe came into existence cannot be answered. Buddhists do not believe in a creator god, so they do not believe that the universe was created by one supreme being. They believe that it has always been here, moving through patterns of beginnings and endings. This will always be the case and people need only realize that all life will involve change. What matters to Buddhists is to try and make sense of the life they live now, using it as an opportunity to find Enlightenment and move closer to nirvana.

THINK ABOUT IT!

4. What do Buddhists believe about life? What effect do these beliefs have on their understanding of the world today?

⊃ The Buddha taught that to endlessly speculate about how the universe arose and when it will end will not lead to a sense of ease and well-being.

In this lesson you will:
- explore Darwin's theory of evolution
- identify the impact of Darwin's ideas
- evaluate some of the religious responses to Darwin's work.

KEY WORDS

Genetic inherited characteristics in animals and plants

Natural selection 'survival of the fittest' – the theory at the heart of evolution

APES OR ANGELS?

According to modern **genetic** science, 99% of the genetic information found in a human being can also be found in an ape. Apes are our nearest relatives. We first began to understand this genetic link because of an English scientist called Charles Darwin (1809–82), who developed the theory of evolution.

The idea of evolution was a very old one. In the fourth century CE, the Christian writer Augustine had written, 'After all, cells in due course gave birth to all things.' Augustine had in turn been influenced by Greek writers. Darwin brought the idea of evolution into sharp focus in the nineteenth century.

WHO WAS CHARLES DARWIN?

Between 1831 and 1836, Darwin made a round-the-world journey on the *HMS Beagle* as a research scientist. By examining the animal and insect life in different countries, especially South America, he came to the conclusion that all living things had adapted to their environment over a period of time.

At the time, most Christians believed that the forms of animals were unchangeable since they had been planned and made by God, as recorded in the Book of Genesis in the Jewish and Christian scriptures. However, Darwin suggested that animals could change or evolve from primitive species over a period of time through a process called **natural selection**. By this process, those animals that were best suited or adapted to an environment would have the best chance of survival. For example, birds that fly quickly are better able to escape predators and reach food than birds that fly slowly. Darwin suggested that some species survive better because those members which are better adapted to the environment are more likely to produce offspring who will then share their parents' advantageous characteristics. Natural selection is therefore also referred to as 'survival of the fittest'.

Charles Darwin's theory of evolution caused much argument.

THINK ABOUT IT!

1. How does the theory of evolution tie in with what you have learned so far about creation?

According to Darwin's theory of evolution, fish adapted over time by developing legs and the ability to breathe air, moving onto the Earth and eventually becoming lizards.

HOW DID RELIGIOUS PEOPLE RESPOND?

Many Christians disagreed with Darwin's theory of evolution because it seemed to deny the work of a creator God. Darwin himself was uneasy about sharing what he had discovered. He felt that some people would think he was proving that Christianity was wrong. In his book *On the Origin of Species* (1859), Darwin suggested that God could be behind the whole process of evolution.

Some people have suggested that Darwin wrote this in order to keep the Christian Church happy. He was probably aware that if he stated his theory more openly, it would cause great controversy. Perhaps Darwin was beginning to believe that evolution did not need a designer God to help it along. Either way, it was over a decade before Darwin published his book *The Descent of Man* (1871), in which he suggested that human beings had evolved from apes.

Many Christians disliked Darwin's theory of evolution, for several reasons.

- If humans were still evolving, how did this fit in with the idea of a creator God who had made humans in His own image? It led to the conclusion that human beings were like any other animals. Did this mean that human life was not really valuable?

- If humans were simply animals, what did morality and religion matter? Were laws such as the Ten Commandments irrelevant? Surely animals could never expect to live up to those rules?

THE IMPACT OF DARWIN'S THEORY

Over the decades, the theory of evolution has affected not only how people see the origins of the human race but also its development. For example, extreme political movements such as the Nazi Party in the 1930s and 1940s used the language of 'survival of the fittest' to suggest that only people fitting their idea of a master race should be allowed to live. Others have used Darwin's theory to justify the idea that the rich and powerful will win through so the poor and vulnerable can be left to naturally die out.

THINK ABOUT IT!

2. Create a spider diagram to show the problems raised by the idea of evolution for some religious people.

3. Do you think that the idea of evolution has to be in conflict with Christian belief? Give reasons for your answers.

4. What might religious people think about the way in which the idea of 'survival of the fittest' has been used to justify the poor treatment of others? Give reasons for your answer.

In this lesson you will:
● investigate the debates raised by the Scopes Trial
● explore some tension between religion and science
● identify the impact of the theory of evolution on society.

KEY WORDS

Intelligent design the belief that there is scientific evidence to support the Genesis story of a creator God

Creation Science the attempt to show that science backs the idea of creation

● WHAT WAS THE SCOPES TRIAL ABOUT?

In March 1925, the state government of Tennessee in the USA passed a law that banned schools from teaching the theory of evolution and ordered that schools only teach the Genesis creation story. A Biology teacher called John Scopes believed that this was wrong and continued to teach the theory of evolution. As a result he was arrested, and his trial attracted international attention.

Scopes' defence lawyer was Clarence Darrow, who was known for taking on impossible cases and winning. The prosecution lawyer was William Jennings Bryan, who was an ex-presidential candidate and had been a friend of Darrow's.

🎧 **Clarence Darrow, the defence lawyer in the 1925 Scopes Trial.**

Darrow argued that the state had no right to pass a law which limited the right of someone to learn or to teach, but Bryan replied that the state had a duty to encourage godly learning.

🎧 **William Jennings Bryan, the prosecution lawyer in the 1925 Scopes Trial.**

The judge ruled that the evidence of scientific experts the defence wished to call was irrelevant. Darrow was unsure what to do to help Scopes, so he called Bryan as an expert witness on the Bible. What follows on page 31 is taken from the court record.

THINK ABOUT IT!

1. Was it right of John Scopes to knowingly break the law? Give reasons for your answer.

2. Write down the names of any other people you can think of who have knowingly broken the law because of their beliefs. Were they right or wrong to do so? Why?

Darrow: Do you believe the Bible to be literally true?
Bryan: I do.
Darrow: Do you believe the book of Joshua when it says the sun stopped?
Bryan: I do.
Darrow: But if the sun stopped, so would life on Earth!
Bryan: It was a miracle.
Darrow: A miracle? Like Jonah being swallowed by a mighty fish?
Bryan: Indeed.
Darrow: You don't know whether it was an ordinary fish or made for the purpose?
Bryan: I don't – only the good Lord does.
Darrow: Do you believe the flood happened, that it was history?

Bryan: I do.
Darrow: When did it happen?
Bryan: I never made a calculation.
Darrow: What do you think?
Bryan: I don't think about things I don't think about.
Darrow: Do you think about things you do think about?
Bryan: Er...
Darrow: And how long were the days of creation?
Bryan: Well, the Hebrew word for 'days' can mean a period of time.
Darrow: Start talking like that and I'd come to believe that you don't believe in the literal truth of the Bible. When you start playing with words, how can you take the Bible seriously?

The jury found John Scopes guilty but the Judge ruled that Scopes had to pay a $100 fine (equivalent to £25 today), which was the lowest possible fine he could give. However, the law remained in force until 1968. John Scopes left teaching and went to Texas, where he became an oil man and died a millionaire!

THINK ABOUT IT!

3. Write a speech for John Scopes to give at the end of the trial, explaining why he broke the law.

● THE DEBATE CONTINUES...

Today, in many states in the USA, school textbooks must teach the story of creation as well as the theory of evolution. Over eighty years on from the Scopes Trial, a substantial number of Americans continue to believe that the theory of evolution is not scientifically viable and that the world was made in six days by a creator God.

● WHAT IS CREATION SCIENCE?

There are many people who believe that God created the world. However, not everyone who believes that the universe is God's creation shares the same belief about how it was created. One theory that some people support today is called **intelligent design**.

The modern theory of intelligent design was developed in the 1980s. It maintains that whilst evolution is a good scientific theory there is also scientific evidence for a designer. Intelligent design states that the complexity of the Earth can only be explained by the existence of a creator God. Supporters of **Creation Science** argue that people who believe in the theory of evolution do so not because of scientific evidence, but because of faith. Creation Scientists point out that the theory of evolution has not been proved any more than any of the religious creation stories.

THINK ABOUT IT!

4. 'People who believe in evolution are not trusting in science but making an act of faith'. What might a person who believes in Creation Science mean by this? Do you agree? Give reasons for your answer showing that you have thought about it from more than one point of view.

5. Do you think that science lessons should contain ideas about both evolution theory and creation theory? Give reasons for your answer, showing that you have thought about it from more than one point of view.

In this lesson you will:
- explore scientific theories about the end of the world
- evaluate whether the end of the world might be caused by human action.

KEY WORDS

Big Crunch theory that the universe will one day collapse back in on itself

HOW WILL IT ALL END?

> 'This is the way the world ends,
> Not with a bang but a whimper.'
>
> *T.S. Eliot (1888–1965)*

Using Google™ as a search engine, a researcher discovered 15,700,000 references to the end of the world on the Internet. By the time you read this, there will probably be many more. Some of these websites are scientific, some of them are religious, and some of them are personal ideas of individuals as to how the world might end.

The philosopher and scientist John Leslie, writing in *The End of the World* (1996), suggested several ways in which the world could end:
- pollution ends all life
- the Earth goes out of the orbit of the Sun
- a comet hits the planet.

Will the Earth explode?

Will an asteroid hit the planet?

Will pollution end life?

THINK ABOUT IT!

1. Look at John Leslie's suggestions for how the world will end. Do you think any of these might actually happen?

2. Do you think the world will end? If so, how do you think it will happen? Give reasons for your answer.

● A BIG CRUNCH?

Some scientists believe that the end of the world will most likely happen with what they call a **Big Crunch**. The Big Bang, the cosmic explosion that some scientists believe started all life in the universe, still has consequences today. Matter and space continue to expand, this suggests that at some point the cosmos will eventually reach a point where it collapses back in on itself – rather like a balloon deflating. As a consequence, all matter will be squashed back into the microscopic particles that actually started the Big Bang in the first place. Other scientists believe that the universe will go on expanding forever.

Scientists are divided as to what happens after the Big Crunch: some believe that there will be another Big Bang and the cosmos will again come into existence, but most believe that the Big Crunch will be the end of everything.

Not every end of the world theory provides a scientific explanation of the universe ending.

- Some focus on the way that humanity uses and abuses the environment. The film *The Day After Tomorrow* (2004) showed how the end of the world could come about by the actions of humanity in allowing environmental pollution and global warming to develop. The film showed how environmental damage could lead to rapid climate change, causing extreme weather with flooding in some areas and the start of a new ice age in others. The burning of fossil fuels and the destruction of the rain forests (once described as the lungs of the Earth) could potentially end human life on the planet.

- Life on the planet could also be threatened by the use of atomic and nuclear weapons, which can cause the devastation of life by radiation.

- Other scientists have speculated that an asteroid could collide with the Earth.

Many religions teach that human beings are responsible for the planet and its future, so they must live and act appropriately to make sure that they are not judged by God or find karma working against them.

Big Bang – a cosmic explosion

Matter and space are still expanding after the Big Bang

Cosmos will eventually collapse and squash back into the particles that started the Big Bang

🎧 **The Big Crunch could see the end of all things according to some scientists.**

> As a Humanist I believe that we should try to do all we can to protect the planet, but we should do this as an act of love towards our fellow human beings, including our descendants.

Kerrie

THINK ABOUT IT!

3. a) What do you think are the greatest threats to life on Earth? Represent your ideas on a spider diagram.
   b) Now underline the threats that are caused by humans.
   c) Extend your spider diagram by adding solutions to these problems.

4. Compare your spider diagram with a partner's. How are your threats and solutions similar and how are they different?

In this lesson you will:
● raise questions about religious ideas of the end of the world
● reflect on how ideas about the end of the world might influence the behaviour of believers in the present.

As you discovered in the previous lesson, there are many different theories about how the world might end. For some religious people, beliefs about the end of the world are an important guide to how they should live today.

For some, the prospect of the end of the world holds the comfort of paradise. For others, the challenge of living today includes trying to make the Earth more like this perfect place and time that will be revealed. Yet in order to reach this time of peace, many people believe that there will first be a time of great upheaval, marked by wars, natural disasters and evil.

Endings can be positive and negative.

WHAT MIGHT A CHRISTIAN BELIEVE?

● Many Christians believe that the final book of the New Testament, Revelation, is important because it teaches about the end of the world. Revelation looks forward to a time of a new heaven and a new Earth. Many Christians also believe that Jesus will come again – the **Second Coming** – and that with his arrival the world will be transformed and suffering will disappear.

● As well as the book of Revelation, there are passages in the Gospels which show that Jesus thought about how the world might end. He told stories such as the parable of the sheep and the goats, in which he described an 'end to the age', when history comes to an end and God comes to rule. In the Gospels, Jesus had looked forward to this time.

'Then the Son of Man will appear, coming in clouds with great power and glory. He will send the angels out to the four corners of the Earth to gather God's chosen people from one end of the world to the other.'

The Bible, Mark 13: 26–7

- For some groups or sects, the idea of Jesus' Second Coming is a major part of their teaching. One of these is the Jehovah's Witnesses. This sect teaches that Jesus' Second Coming took place in 1914 and that the Last Days, as predicted in the Bible, then began. They believe that at some point in the future, God will allow everyone to see what the government of God will look like on Earth and in heaven, although only an elect, a specially chosen group of 144,000, will live in heaven forever.

- Some Christians are not sure if there will be a literal return of Jesus, saying that perhaps the events of the Resurrection and of Pentecost (when Christians believe that God gave the gift of the Holy Spirit) were Jesus' Second Coming. If this is so, then thinking about the end of the world becomes difficult. Many Christians simply say that, however the world ends, God's purposes will have been fulfilled.

- Some Christians believe in an event they call the **Rapture**, when all Christian believers will be transported to heaven leaving all non-Christians behind.

 Many Christians believe that Christ will return to earth to reign in power.

THINK ABOUT IT!

1. How important do you think the idea of the Second Coming of Jesus is to Christians? Give your reasons, showing why you think it might and might not be important.

2. What effect do you think that believing in the Second Coming will have on Christians and the way they live today?

● WHAT MIGHT A BUDDHIST BELIEVE?

In contrast, Buddhists see the end of the world very differently. They see time as an endless circle where things repeat themselves, including universes coming in and out of existence. For Buddhists, the ultimate aim of human life is not to survive the end of the world or be accepted into heaven, but to realize nirvana now, the state of perfect peace. Buddhists believe that every beginning has its ending contained within it, since all life is in a constant state of change. Worlds are always ending and they are always beginning.

THINK ABOUT IT!

3. Explain Buddhist ideas about the end of the world. How might they help people to deal with the problems they face in life?

WHAT THE TASK IS ALL ABOUT:

1. Write the script for a TV mock trial: 'God in the Dock'

Or

2. You are speaking in a debate defending or challenging the following statement:

'Having a scientific view of the origins of the universe does not necessarily rule out belief in God.' Write your argument using the information in this chapter.

WHAT YOU NEED TO DO TO COMPLETE THE TASK:

1. Identify the witnesses that you will call from chapter 2 (these might include Paley, Dawkins, Darwin, Scopes, a member of the Hindu faith, a member of the Sanema tribe).

Write the questions they will be asked and make notes about how they will answer them.

You are the judge! At the end you will need to sum up and give a verdict, based on the evidence, on whether God was involved in the creation of the world or not.

This could be done as a group activity and then staged in your RE lesson or as an assembly. Make sure you can identify everyone's contribution if you do it as a group task.

Or

2. Choose whether you will defend or challenge the statement and draw up your arguments using the information in the chapter. Remember, you will be challenged so you must be able to show evidence for your arguments.

When you have completed the task you could run a real class or year group debate with people proposing and seconding the motion and being questioned by the audience.

HINTS AND TIPS

- Learn the key words in this chapter and their meaning.
- Make sure that you have a good grasp of the religious and non-religious ideas mentioned in this chapter.
- Make sure that you always write answers which show a variety of opinions on a topic.
- Include both scientific and religious ideas in your answers.

TO ACHIEVE	YOU WILL NEED TO
Level 4	Show that you understand the reasons for different religious and non-religious beliefs about the origins of the universe. Use the ideas raised in this chapter to help you reflect on your own answers to the questions raised.
Level 5	Explain how writings and teachings of religious and scientific theories are used to support arguments about the origin of the universe. Explain your own views about the relationship between religion and science.
Level 6	Use the information in this chapter to help you interpret and present arguments about religious and scientific views of the origin of the universe. Explain the reasons behind your own views about the relationship between science and religion.
Level 7	Show that you have analysed the evidence and presented a clearly argued case, using a good religious and scientific vocabulary. Pose your own questions and explain your views on the relationship between religion and science, giving well argued reasons and examples.

SCIENCE AND ETHICS

THE BIGGER PICTURE

In this chapter you will learn about some controversial issues in science and some of the religious responses to these. You will explore issues such as cloning, transplants and IVF. You will seek to understand the scientific issues and the religious and non-religious responses to them.

WHAT?

You will:
- understand key terms such as 'cloning', 'organ donation', 'IVF', 'quality of life' and 'sanctity of life'
- explore scientific and moral issues in these areas and the religious responses to them
- reflect on the relationship between belief and scientific research and action.

HOW?

By:
- investigating issues surrounding cloning, IVF and genetic engineering
- examining how animals should be cared for
- exploring issues surrounding heart and other transplants
- analysing how religious and non-religious ideas influence science
- expressing your own views about the use and abuse of science.

WHY?

Because:
- it is important to understand what it means to be part of a society which values science and how religious and non-religious responses can help science to develop
- you will develop the ability to think for yourself and form your own opinions about some controversial issues
- religious people respond in different ways to science and the moral issues it raises, and it is important to understand these beliefs and how they are helpful to people.

KEY IDEAS

- Science and religion are not always in agreement about some issues.
- Cloning, genetic engineering and IVF play an important part in today's world, and religious people hold different views about the ethical implications of these issues.
- Scientific discoveries often raise moral and religious issues that need to be explored.
- Some religious beliefs affect the way people treat the world around them and their attitudes to scientific discoveries, for example, the Hindu belief in ahimsa affects the way they treat animals.
- The Tower of Babel story gives Jews and Christians a picture of how humans' arrogance about technology can be destructive.
- Science and religion both try to understand the world around them.

KEY WORDS

Science	In Vitro Fertilization (IVF)
Embryo	Infertile
Cloning	DNA
Genetic inheritance	Genetic engineering
Sanctity of life	Pagan
Animal experimentation	Stewardship
Dominion	Ahimsa
Transplant	Resurrection
Fatwa	Xenotransplantation
Blood transfusion	

Science and religion both try to understand the world around them but do not always agree with each other.

In this lesson you will:
- explore how science tries to get to the truth
- investigate the relationship between religion and science
- form your own opinions about whether conflict between religion and science is justified.

KEY WORDS

Science study of the physical, biological and chemical processes of the universe

● WHAT IS SCIENCE?

Since the beginning of time, human beings have tried to make sense of their own bodies, the planet they live on and the universe around them. People have believed that they can make sense of life whether through religion or **science**.

Science stems from the belief that the world has an order and a purpose to it, a sense that, for some, is reinforced by religion. Many early scientists felt that they were trying to understand something that had been planned by God.

🎧 **The German astronomer Johannes Kepler (1571–1630), who said 'I was merely thinking God's thoughts after him'.**

THINK ABOUT IT!

1. What really surprises you about the universe? Make a list of at least three things. Compare your list with a partner.

2. **a)** Write a definition of the word 'science'.
   b) Compare your definition to the dictionary, what are the similarities? Are there any differences?

3. Look at the caption under the picture of Kepler. What do you think he meant by this?

Today, scientists try to understand the universe by applying certain principles.

1 *Scientists generalize.* Scientists try to find the basic laws of nature. For example, all objects with mass experience the attractive force of gravity.

2 *Scientists investigate.* Scientists conduct observable experiments in order to find out how things work. Scientists look for repeatable results because they know that a single observation might be mistaken.

TRANSPLANTS
RELIGION
?
CLONING

?
SCIENCE
I.V.F.
?
?
GENETIC ENGINEERING

4 *Scientists develop theories.* A theory is when a scientist puts forward evidence about something to explain why or how it happens. Theories can be developed and added to with time. For example, the evolutionary theories of Charles Darwin (see Chapter 2, pages 28–9) have developed and changed as science has learned more about the evolutionary process.

3 *Scientists must keep up to date.* In other words, science has to constantly update its findings as new information is discovered about the universe. For example, scientists once believed that the sun goes round the earth, but this idea has since been proved wrong.

● **CAN RELIGION AND SCIENCE WORK TOGETHER?**

Religious people sometimes ask similar questions to those asked by scientists. For example, questions about why the world is the way it is. But do science and religion come up with similar answers or different ones? Some religious people see science as an attempt to ignore God's revelation, to replace this given knowledge with human answers. Others see science as a way of understanding the universe in a different but complimentary way to religion.

THINK ABOUT IT!

4. List some questions that science and religion might have in common.

Many religious people acknowledge that science and religion work in a similar way.

- In both, people make generalizations in order to discover an order: for example, the belief in a created universe or one that happened by chance.
- In both, people investigate the universe, because although it might appear mysterious, they expect it to work according to certain principles or rules.
- Scientists carry out experiments in order to arrive at the truth. Religious people might also say that the only way to the truth is by personally investigating or experiencing things: for example, by taking part in religious practices such as prayer or meditation.

Religion has asked science some tough questions, about the rights and wrongs of its discoveries. For example, just because we can clone animals does it make it right to do so?

Some scientific discoveries have proved difficult for religious people to accept. When Nicolaus Copernicus (1473–1543) and Galileo Galilei (1564–1642) showed that the Earth went round the Sun rather than the other way round, some religious people felt this to be an attack on the special relationship humanity had with God (whereby the Earth was at the centre of the universe). Similarly, when Charles Darwin (1809–82) put forward his theory of evolution, some religious people saw this as an attack on the idea of God as creator (see Chapter 2, pages 29–31).

However, not all religious people agree with asking questions about the universe. For example, a fundamentalist Muslim or Christian might argue that everything has been created by God and to ask questions is inappropriate. For some Buddhists what matters is not understanding but the experience of Enlightenment.

THINK ABOUT IT!

5. Do you think science and religion need to be in conflict? Give reasons for your answer.

In this lesson you will:
- investigate IVF, cloning and genetic engineering
- reflect on some of the practical and moral issues raised by them
- reflect on some of the religious responses to the moral issues
- explore the implications of these discoveries for people today.

KEY WORDS

In Vitro Fertilization (IVF) process of fertilizing an egg in a test tube before replacing it in the womb

Embryo unborn offspring

Infertile not able to conceive

Cloning inserting an adult's genetic information into an egg cell to produce an offspring which is genetically identical to its parent

DNA deoxyribonucleic acid: the building block of cell life

Genetic inheritance the genes humans receive from their parents

Genetic engineering manipulation of genetic material

Scientific discoveries often provoke moral and religious debate. Three important discoveries of the twentieth century that have done just that are:
- IVF
- cloning
- genetic engineering.

In this lesson you will examine briefly these discoveries from a scientific point of view. Over the next lessons you will have the opportunity to reflect on the religious and moral debates they raise.

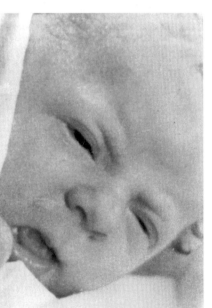

Louise Brown, the first test tube baby. IVF has helped many couples conceive.

● IVF: BABIES IN A TEST TUBE

In England in the summer of 1978, Louise Brown was the first baby to be born using IVF. **In Vitro Fertilization (IVF)** is when a woman's egg is fertilized in a test tube (*in vitro* means 'in glass') using sperm from the father, rather than inside the mother's body. The resulting **embryo** is then implanted in the mother's womb. This is called Artificial Insemination by the Husband (AIH). Thousands of children have been conceived in this way since 1978.

Other forms of IVF treatment available today include:
- AID – Artificial Insemination by Donor. This is when a woman's egg is fertilized in a test tube using sperm from a donor father, who isn't known to the woman.
- When a couple are trying for a baby and the woman is **infertile**, the eggs necessary for fertilization can be donated by another woman. The donor eggs are then fertilized using the infertile partner's sperm and the resulting embryo is implanted in the infertile woman's womb.

In 1982, a government report called the Warnock Report recommended some guidelines for IVF:

- infertility is a good reason for IVF
- human embryos developed in this technique are not to be used for general research
- any research on the embryo has to be performed within fourteen days of fertilization
- only licensed doctors can perform IVF treatment.

These guidelines were made law in 1990.

THINK ABOUT IT!

1. Explain the following:
   a) AIH
   b) AID
   c) egg donation
   d) implanting an embryo.

   What moral and/or religious problems might each raise? Why?

NEVER ALONE WITH A CLONE

Cloning is the process of taking a cell or genetic material and creating life from it.

In 1996, scientists at the Roslin Institute in Scotland created Dolly the sheep using cells taken from another sheep. This is an example of reproductive cloning. Although such a clone might be identical in genetic terms, it may be different overall due to environmental influences, just as identical twins can have very different characteristics though they share a genetic make up.

GENETIC ENGINEERING: CRACKING THE CODE

The Human Genome project was set up in 1990 to decode and map the **DNA** that makes up the human body. The research has had significant implications. For example, it might now be possible to spot inherited diseases such as Huntingdon's disease and multiple sclerosis by looking at a person's **genetic inheritance**; the defective genes could then be corrected before the disease develops. It is now possible for parents to determine the sex of their children using **genetic engineering**.

Genetic engineering is also used on plants and animals. For example, it is possible to genetically modify plants so they become more resistant to extremes of weather, grow in greater supply, are more resistant to attacks from insects, and taste better for human consumers.

MORAL ISSUES

However, the question of genetic engineering is not simply about avoiding illness and increasing the food supply – it also raises important moral and for some, religious questions which people must think through for themselves.

> How do you decide what an illness or a disability is?

> Should humans be reduced to just another thing that is manufactured according to demand?

> Will the cloning of embryos provide long-term solutions for thousands of people with genetically inherited conditions?

> What if genetically modified plants cross-breed with other plants by pollination and develop into 'superweeds'? Are humans playing God?

> Will interfering with the genetic make-up of foods make them less tasty or cause them to become a source of disease? What is the environmental effect?

Dolly the sheep and her creator. Should we create new life by cloning?

THINK ABOUT IT!

2. What moral problems are caused by the cloning of:
   a) animals?
   b) human material, such as stem cells?

   Give reasons for your answers.

THINK ABOUT IT!

3. If you could change anything about the human body using genetic engineering, what would you change? What problems might arise if you tried to do this?

4. 'Genetically modified food provides a solution to the problem of human hunger.' Do you agree? Give reasons for your answer, showing that you have thought about it from more than one point of view.

In this lesson you will:
- investigate different Christian responses to cloning, IVF and genetic engineering
- evaluate the ways in which religious belief affects people's responses to these issues.

KEY WORDS

Sanctity of life the idea that all life comes from God and is therefore holy

WHAT DO CHRISTIANS BELIEVE?

For Christians, the issues of IVF, cloning and genetic engineering raise a number of important questions. Below are some key Christian responses to the issues raised by IVF, cloning and genetic engineering.

God alone should be the ultimate creator of life

According to the book of Genesis, God's natural creation is perfect. Many Catholics therefore believe that because IVF is a scientific technique rather than the natural way to conceive, it is contrary to God's will. Also, by trying to modify plants or other life forms through genetic engineering, scientists are effectively saying that God's creation is in some way defective and lacking.

Many Christians argue that people should allow nature to develop in the way it was intended, and not interfere with it in a way that reflects humanity's selfish and sinful nature.

Selective breeding was experimented with in the nineteenth century. Should you breed a more perfect human being?

Human beings are 'made in the image of God'

Do IVF, cloning and genetic engineering make life something that is created to satisfy human desires rather than a divine miracle? Are they in this way an attack on God?

Some christians might also question how a person created by cloning can reflect the creator God. Will these scientific methods undermine humanity's relationship with God, since God is the creator who made people in God's own image?

God gave humans a soul

Some Christians say that only God can place a soul into a person and that a clone developed by science would not have this unique gift. However, identical twins are in a sense a natural example of cloning, and there has been no debate that only one twin has soul! So perhaps this does not have to be a problem for religious believers.

Other Christians suggest that a human clone would still have their own individual soul that would survive death, though they may wonder what sort of relationship such a person would have with God.

THINK ABOUT IT!

1. What do you think Christians mean when they say that humans are made in the image of God? How do you think this belief might influence their behaviour towards other people?

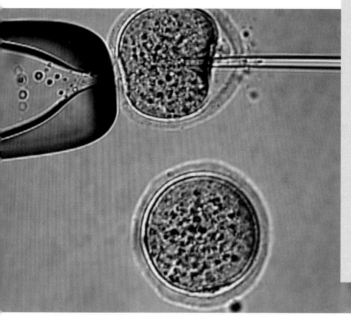

Life is holy

IVF is often unsuccessful. The creation and implantation of an embryo in this way when the risk of miscarriage is high, is against Catholic teachings on the **sanctity of life**.

Artificial Insemination by the Husband (AIH) might be acceptable to some Catholics and Methodists because it allows a childless couple to have a child and is one way in which a husband can show love and care for his wife. However, Artificial Insemination by Donor (AID) is unacceptable to many Christians because it is seen as adultery.

The genetic engineering of cells from embryos is, for some Christians, creating new lives simply to harvest them for use by others. Many Catholics see this practice as abortion in order to help others, and therefore believe it to be fundamentally wrong.

🎧 **Stem cell research has proved controversial because some believe that cells used in such research could have come from embryos.**

THINK ABOUT IT!

2. Choose one of the following statements to discuss as a group.
   a) 'Religion should not interfere with how people conceive.'
   b) 'Human life should only be created in the way God meant it to be.'

   What do you think about the statement? What might a Christian think?
   Give reasons for your answer, showing that you have thought about it from more than one point of view.

3. Write a brief article for a Christian magazine or newspaper reporting one of the following:
   a) the birth of Louise Brown
   b) the discovery of the human genome
   c) the cloning of Dolly the Sheep.

   You might want to include some of the following words and phrases in your article: 'creation', 'the image of God', 'creator', 'all life is holy'.

Everyone is entitled to enjoy a good quality of life

Some Christians argue that people should be free to make their own choices in life. They have concerns that human cloning could make it possible to produce people with certain types of personality or behaviour, thereby limiting their freedom to choose and develop freely. Many Christians believe that people are responsible for their free choices to God and will be judged accordingly – how can clones be judged in this way if they have been manufactured like machines?

Some Christians have suggested that genetic engineering could be used to improve life but should be used only in limited, strictly-controlled circumstances. They point out that genetic engineering does not provide the solution to all the planet's problems, but might help in limited ways. For example, whilst using genetically engineered food could help with the problem of famine, some Christians argue that there is enough food in the world to feed everyone already if only people knew how to share.

In this lesson you will:
- investigate Buddhist, Pagan and Humanist responses to the creation of life issues
- analyse the moral issues involved in the creation of life.

KEY WORDS

Pagan a belief in many gods and that nature should be worshipped

● BUDDHIST RESPONSES TO THE CREATION OF LIFE

Buddhists have mixed responses to issues of genetic engineering, IVF and cloning. Some see them as tampering with nature and going against the natural order of things. However, there is also a strong belief in Buddhism that it is the intentions behind actions that are most important: if the intention is honest and good, it might make the action acceptable.

Buddhists who disagree with genetic engineering and cloning might argue that:
- by interfering with nature, people might also affect the natural law of karma. Karma teaches that all actions have consequences. If an action is considered to be tampering with nature it might result in negative consequences
- IVF and genetic engineering could be considered to break the first moral precept: avoid taking life. For example, the process of genetic engineering and cloning can lead to the destruction of living human beings
- their teachings advise against developing strong desires (attachments) towards things. One danger with IVF, cloning and genetic engineering is that people can develop strong desires about the people they are creating, like objects that can be bought and sold.

Buddhists who agree with genetic engineering, IVF and cloning, or are indifferent to them, might believe that:
- the most important thing, in all situations, is the careful consideration of the intentions of actions. For example, if the intention of genetic engineering and cloning is to save lives this might make it acceptable
- it is impossible to tell when 'life' starts. Some Buddhists believe life starts at conception but others believe life can start anywhere between conception and birth. Without being able to tell when life begins it is difficult to say whether procedures such as IVF do actually break any of the moral precepts.

Many people have protested against genetically modified food.

THINK ABOUT IT!

1. Think about why a Buddhist might question the use of genetic engineering. What are the strong parts of their argument? What are the weak parts of their argument?

● HOW MIGHT A PAGAN RESPOND?

The Pagan Federation, a group that represents many **Pagans**, describes itself as believing in many gods and being a nature-worshipping religion. The Pagan love of nature means that they show reverence for nature and the cycle of life and death. Pagans, therefore, question scientists who wish to play with nature by creating life artificially.

For Pagans, each person is responsible for their own sense of right and wrong. This individual conscience arises from each person's true nature and is dependent on remaining in harmony with nature. Pagans might argue that it is because people in modern society are out of touch with nature that they seek to influence nature artificially, for example, playing with the human reproductive processes through IVF, cloning and genetic engineering. Many Pagans have been involved in protests against genetically modified food, which they see as being against the natural way of things and having the potential to harm the environment.

Pagans believe that people should show deep respect for all life.

● WHAT A HUMANIST MIGHT THINK...

Because Humanists do not believe that deities will help humanity to solve its problems, most Humanists think that people should use their knowledge and understanding to solve problems and make life happier. Many Humanists acknowledge that science can help people to deal with some of the great questions of life and overcome problems.

However, Humanists acknowledge that science can get it wrong and be harmful to society. When considering whether IVF, cloning and genetic engineering are good for humanity, many Humanists therefore believe that the pros and cons of each should be thoroughly and openly debated first. Humanists argue that the more informed we are about the issues of IVF, cloning and genetic engineering, the more able we will be to make decisions regarding them that are good for society as a whole.

THINK ABOUT IT!

2. What do you think are the strong points of Humanist arguments? What do you think are the weak points of their arguments?

THINK ABOUT IT!

3. Is it really possible for humans not to alter the natural world around them?

4. 'There are more benefits to be gained from genetic engineering than negatives'. Do you agree? How might a Buddhist, Pagan or Humanist respond to this statement? Give reasons for your answers.

5. 'Believing in a god who will judge you will make you more likely to care for the environment'. How might a Buddhist, Pagan or Humanist respond to this? What do you think? Give reasons for your answers.

In this lesson you will:
- reflect on the moral debates about the treatment of animals in scientific experiments
- analyse religious understandings of the issues surrounding animal experiments
- express your own responses to the issues raised.

KEY WORDS

Animal experimentation to perform scientific research using animals

Stewardship human responsibility to look after the world and everything in it; looking after something so it can be passed onto the next generation

Dominion control over or responsibility for the Earth

Ahimsa non-violence, respect for life

PROTECTORS OR TERRORISTS?

For several years, the laboratories of Huntingdon Life Sciences have been the focus for demonstrations and protests against **animal experimentation**. This is because the government has allowed the company to perform experiments on animals in order to help with medical and other scientific research. Many of those protesting about Huntingdon Life Sciences have used non-violent methods. However, some protestors have used violent methods and have threatened people working there.

One of the key questions for scientists is whether animals should be used in experiments. In the past, some companies were happy to employ scientists to test cosmetic products, such as lipstick and shampoo, on animals. They saw nothing wrong with animal experimentation.

Today, many companies will not test their products on animals. The success of the Body Shop, which has campaigned against animal experimentation since 1990, suggests that many people would prefer that products were not tested on animals.

Should animals have the same rights as humans?

THINK ABOUT IT!

1. Do you think animals and humans have equal rights? Do you think that animals are the responsibility of humans?

2. Do the protestors have a right to threaten people working at Huntingdon Life Sciences?

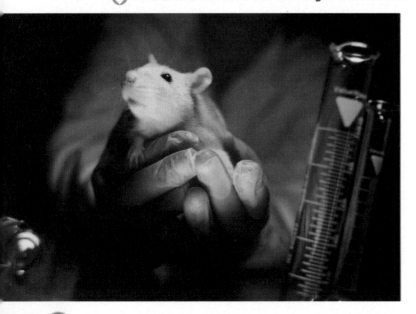

Many people protest against animal experimentation, this has sometimes led to violence.

IS MEDICAL TESTING ACCEPTABLE?

People often have mixed feelings about animal experimentation. On the one hand, animal experimentation can be seen as worthwhile if it helps us to understand the way a disease works and to find a cure. On the other hand, using animals to test cosmetic products might be seen as pointless cruelty if such testing can be safely carried out on humans.

Both religious and non-religious people face difficult questions about whether the use of animals in experiments is ever acceptable.

For centuries, most people believed that animals were inferior to humans and therefore did not deserve much respect or any rights. Religious people sometimes said that since animals were made by God, they were designed to meet our every need, so we need not feel guilty about how we treated them. However, many other people argue that we should treat animals with care and respect. They say that animals are entitled to rights as much as human beings are.

Does performing an experiment on an animal really help us to understand what might happen to a human being? For example, penicillin kills rats, but it has been one of the greatest life savers for humans.

Although animals such as the chimp are genetically similar to humans, they are not identical and so an experiment performed on chimps could give misleading results.

Animals feel pain – should we inflict pain on them?

THINK ABOUT IT!

3. What experiments are acceptable to perform on animals? Which are unacceptable? Give reasons for your answers.

WHAT MIGHT A CHRISTIAN SAY?

Many Christians believe that God created all life for humanity to be **stewards** or guardians over, so it is therefore a human responsibility to respect and care for animals. Other Christians believe that God gave humanity **dominion** or power over animals, including how to use them and deciding whether they should live or die. This belief is based on the book of Genesis, which describes how God puts humanity in charge of all creation.

'Then God said, "And now we will make human beings; they will be like us and resemble us. They will have power over the fish, the birds and all animals, domestic and wild, large and small."'

The Bible, Genesis 1: 26

The Bible also describes how God gave humans the right to name animals, which shows the authority that people have over them.

THE HINDU VIEW

Hindus believe that animals are holy and have a soul. In particular, the cow is considered sacred and holds a special place in Hindu culture. It is believed to have been the companion to both Krishna and Shiva and today the selling of beef is banned in many Indian holy cities and areas.

Hindus believe in **ahimsa** meaning non-violence or the idea that no harm should be done to any living thing. Most Hindus, therefore, avoid supporting any scientific experiment which could cause harm to an animal. Many Hindus also believe that the abuse of animals will negatively affect their karma.

THINK ABOUT IT!

4. Create a spider diagram to show the Christian and Hindu attitudes towards animals. In a different coloured pen, add your own views to the diagram.

5. Using the information on your diagram write a response to the following statement: 'Many people argue that the ill-treatment of animals is caused, in part, by the religious belief that God created animals and put humans in charge of them.'

6. 'If we followed the Hindu teaching of ahimsa we would have missed out on many medical advances'. How might a Hindu answer this? What do you think?

In this lesson you will:
- investigate the procedures and issues raised by organ transplantation
- explore moral and religious questions raised by organ transplants.

Imagine you are told that your child is going to die. What would you be prepared to do in order to help them?

A FATHER'S STORY

Brian was told that his daughter would die unless she was given part of a liver. However, there was no donor liver available, so Brian asked the doctors to take some of his own liver in order to help his daughter. It saved her life. It also meant that for many months Brian was in pain and at risk of infection. Today, seven years on, Brian and his daughter are both healthy and well.

ORGAN DONATION

In 1905, the first organ **transplant** took place when a cornea was replaced in an eye. Today, we are able to transplant hearts, kidneys and many other organs.

Many people have joined the NHS Organ Donor Register. This is a confidential, computerised database which holds the wishes of more than twelve million people. The register is used after a person has died to help establish whether they wanted to donate, and, if so, which organs. Go to www.heinemann.co.uk/hotlinks (express code 7355P) to find out more.

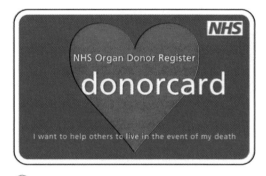

The NHS Organ Donor Register was established in 1995 and is the best way to register wishes about donation. Cards can get lost or damaged and the person may not be carrying one when they are taken to hospital. Being on the register is a more permanent way of expressing your wishes.

CHRISTIAN PERSPECTIVES

In the past, some Christians believed that they should be buried with all their organs intact, so that at the time of the **resurrection** their bodies would be complete. They believed that because God had made them complete, it was not right to interfere with God's purpose. This belief meant that some Christians did not agree with organ transplantation. Today, many Christians argue that it does not matter if the physical body is not intact at burial, since they believe God will remake bodies at the time of the resurrection. Other Christians view the gift of organ donation as a very visible expression of the teaching of Jesus to show practical care for others.

> 'The greatest love a person can have for his friends is to give his life for them.'
>
> *The Bible, John 14: 13*

THINK ABOUT IT!

1. What are your views on organ donation?

   Would you be prepared to donate an organ to help a family member, or a stranger?

A MUSLIM VIEW

Some Muslims believe that a human body needs to be buried complete, as Allah had made him or her, so that the person can enter Paradise. However, in 1995, the Muslim Council of Great Britain issued a **fatwa** (ruling) stating their support for organ donation and encouraging Muslims to join the NHS Organ Donor Register. The Council argued that Allah would want Muslims to help those in need – and that if organ donation is made as an act of love towards others, then Allah would restore the donated organ in the next world.

HUMANIST PERSPECTIVES

For Humanists, the most important issue in the question of organ donation is the maintenance of life. Since Humanists do not believe in an afterlife, they do not have concerns about the body being intact at death. Instead, many Humanists argue that the best way to help others in the future is by donating organs upon death or when the need for donation arises. Whilst many Humanists encourage people to join the NHS Organ Donor Register, they also believe that the decision to donate organs is a matter of personal choice.

🎧 **Should only human organs be transplanted into humans?**

WHAT IS XENOTRANSPLANTATION?

Further moral questions concern the transplanting of animal organs to humans, known as **xenotransplantation**. There are not always enough human organs available for donation. Xenotransplantation has increasingly become a possibility for people who desperately need a donor organ in order to survive. This raises the question of whether animals should be bred solely for the purpose of organ donation.

Critics of xenotransplantation point to the high risk of the animal organ being rejected by the human recipient. Others argue that since modern technology can produce cloned or substitute organs, such as electric hearts, these should be used instead of animal organs.

Some religious people question whether animals should be used in this way. They argue that God did not create animals for 'spare-part surgery', and that it is more appropriate to use human organs since God designed them to be used by humans. It could therefore be considered religiously offensive for a Muslim or Jew to be offered organs from animals. However, for Jews human life is paramount and they might therefore consider xenotransplantation if a Rabbi thinks it is appropriate.

BLOOD TRANSFUSIONS

Some religious movements are against the use of donor blood, which is used during operations. The Jehovah's Witnesses do not have **blood transfusions** as they believe this breaks the Biblical principle that no one should drink blood. There have been occasions when hospitals have had to go to court to secure the right to a blood transfusion in order to help a patient who belongs to the Jehovah's Witnesses, who otherwise would have died for refusing donor blood.

THINK ABOUT IT!

2. How are Christian, Muslim and Humanist views of organ donation similar? How are they different?

THINK ABOUT IT!

3. Do you think xenotransplantation should be allowed? What might be the plus and minus points of this idea?

    Record your thoughts using two lists, then share your ideas with a partner.

4. Imagine that a Jehovah's Witness pupil is in need of a blood transfusion as a result of an accident. What do you think the hospital should do? Give reasons for your answer, showing that you have thought about it from more than one point of view.

In this lesson you will:
● explore the stories of *Frankenstein* and the Tower of Babel
● investigate some of the moral dimensions of science
● reflect on the interaction between religion and science.

Many stories have been written about the abuses of science, when humans 'play God' with disastrous consequences. One of the most famous of these stories is *Frankenstein* by Mary Shelley (1797–1851), which was written when she was just eighteen years old. The story tells of a young scientist called Victor Frankenstein who creates a monster from the remains of dead bodies. The monster eventually escapes from Frankenstein, going on the run and killing a young child.

Frankenstein's monster shows how science can go wrong.

● ARE SCIENTISTS PLAYING GOD?

Humanity is capable of achieving almost impossible goals through science.
● Science has theories about how the universe began, the laws of existence, and what will happen at the end of the universe.
● Science has discovered a great deal about how the mind and body works, and provided remarkable breakthroughs in medicine that have saved many lives.
● Genetic engineering and the mapping of the human genome mean that science holds the key to influencing the development of the human race, as well as all animal and plant life on the planet.
● Scientists have also created weapons of mass destruction that are capable of making all life on the planet extinct.

● BRINGING BRICKS TO BABEL

Some Christians, when thinking about science, refer to the story of the Tower of Babel in the book of Genesis.

THINK ABOUT IT!

1. **a)** In what ways does science benefit society?
   b) In what ways does science have a negative influence on society?
   Make notes in pairs, then give feedback to the class.

'Then [the people] said, "Come, let us build ourselves a city, with a tower that reaches to the heavens, so that we may make a name for ourselves and not be scattered over the face of the whole earth."

But the Lord … said, "If as one people speaking the same language they have begun to do this, then nothing they plan to do will be impossible for them. Come, let us go down and confuse their language so they will not understand each other."

So the Lord scattered them over all the earth, and they stopped building the city. That is why it was called Babel – because the Lord confused the language of the whole world.'

The Bible, Genesis 11: 1–9

The Tower of Babel – is this a picture of arrogance?

The Tower of Babel story shows that humanity can become arrogant about the technology it uses. This pride can be destructive because it encourages people to play God – in other words, to think that they have the final say over life or death.

The atomic bomb reduced Hiroshima and Nagasaki to rubble.

WHAT DO RELIGIONS SAY ABOUT SCIENCE?

Religious teachings often suggest that people need a more responsible attitude to science. Many religious people recognise the harm that science could do if not carried out according to a set of moral guidelines: for example, only using science to benefit humanity. Christians might argue that the idea of love for God and humanity should underlie all science.

All religions stress that human actions have consequences, whether karma or facing the judgement of a divine being after death. Religion and morality challenge us to consider the consequences of our actions in a similar way. For example, a scientific breakthrough such as cloning a sheep or building an atomic bomb doesn't necessarily mean that we should use that knowledge. Not all human knowledge will enable humanity to live better lives.

THINK ABOUT IT!

2. Community of enquiry (work as a group to generate and explore your own questions):
    a) What questions would you like to ask about the Tower of Babel story?
    b) What do you think this story means?
    c) Why do you think it is important for Christians?

'I AM BECOME DEATH'

In 1944, the scientist Robert Oppenheimer stood in the Nevada desert watching the explosion of the first atomic bomb. When he saw the effect of the weapon he remarked, 'I am become death', quoting a Hindu scripture The Bhagavad Gita. Oppenheimer realised that he had created something that could cause major loss of life, as was seen when atomic bombs were dropped on the Japanese cities of Hiroshima and Nagasaki in August 1945. Both cities were destroyed and over 130,000 were killed.

THINK ABOUT IT!

3. Choose one of the following statements to discuss in groups. One person from each group will present this to the rest of the class.
    a) 'Science is neither good nor bad. What matters is how people use its discoveries.'
    b) 'Religion has stopped science advancing.'
    Write down:
    ● arguments for
    ● arguments against
    ● arguments which you find most convincing.

4. Write a caption that links all three images in this section. Use ideas from this lesson to help you.

3.8 ASSESSMENT ACTIVITY

WHAT THE TASK IS ALL ABOUT:

In this chapter you have studied the relationship between science, religion and the moral issues raised by new technologies, so the task asks you to think about some of the examples used and the way religions have tried to address them.

1. 'Science should not worry about what is right or wrong – it should just try to do what it can to improve the world. What do you think? Give reasons for your answer.

2. Can religion help scientists to do their work if the scientists are not themselves religious?

WHAT YOU NEED TO DO TO COMPLETE THE TASK:

Task 1

● Think about whether science should worry about issues of right and wrong. Would this limit what people might try to discover? What is the responsibility of science to the general community?

● What do 'right' and 'wrong' mean in this question? Establish what you think is acceptable in terms of scientific progress, and use examples of discoveries from the chapter.

Task 2

● How might religious and non-religious ideas about humanity influence a scientist? Will these influences be positive or negative? Why?

HINTS AND TIPS

● Make sure you understand the following terms and use them correctly: 'morality', 'science', 'IVF', 'genetic engineering', 'cloning'.

● Use religious terms where appropriate.

● Make sure that you always give reasons for your answer and try to give at least two points of view.

● Use examples from at least three of the religious moral issues raised by science in this chapter.

● Think about your answer before you begin to write. You might find it helpful to make notes then write these into full sentences and paragraphs.

● Remember to write a conclusion that sums up your own opinion.

TO ACHIEVE	YOU WILL NEED TO
Level 4	Show a good understanding of the scientific and moral issues you have studied. Make links between religious responses to science, and describe what influences these beliefs and the similarities and differences between them.
Level 5	Show a good understanding of the scientific and moral issues you have studied, and of the similarities and differences between religious responses. Express your own views about scientific, religious and moral issues.
Level 6	Present an informed understanding of the scientific and moral issues you have studied. Explain why there are similarities and differences between the religious responses to scientific issues, and discuss the impact of these responses. Explain your own views about scientific, religious and moral issues.
Level 7	Present a detailed understanding of the scientific religious and moral issues you have studied. Explain why there are similarities and differences between the religious responses to scientific issues, and explain in detail the impact of these responses. Evaluate your own views about scientific, religious and moral issues.

THE SANCTITY OF LIFE

THE BIGGER PICTURE

In this chapter you will explore some of the big moral issues, including the key question 'Is it ever right to destroy or abuse life?' You will start by exploring and reflecting on the idea that life is sacred before tackling such questions as 'Is it ever right to have an abortion?' and 'Do humans have the right to end their own lives?' You are also going to investigate social attitudes to life by considering how people think about sex and family life, and the way in which the elderly are treated.

WHAT?

You will:

- enquire into ideas and beliefs about the sanctity of life
- explore how religious influences about the sanctity of life impact on the lives of religious believers
- reflect on and evaluate the idea that all life is sacred because it is made by God
- express your own views about the sanctity of life and whether it is ever right to interfere with or destroy life.

HOW?

By:

- exploring and suggesting your own ideas about what makes life (and especially human life) special
- investigating religious attitudes towards abortion, euthanasia, sex and the treatment of the elderly
- using empathy, reflection and analysis to evaluate religious ideas from more than one point of view.

WHY?

Because:

- belief about the sanctity of life is a key issue that affects all human beings during their lifetime
- people hold different ideas about the sanctity of life – you need to understand and be respectful of these different views
- you need to be able to express your own views, backing up your opinions with coherent reasons and presenting arguments.

KEY IDEAS

- Issues of life and death are faced by all human beings.
- Most religions believe that all life is created by God and should be respected.
- Many religious people believe that destroying life is a very serious issue.
- Some religious people believe that it can sometimes be acceptable to destroy life, for example if this leads to the end of suffering.
- Other religious people believe that it is rarely, if ever, acceptable to destroy life because only God should decide when life should start or end.

⟳ **How special is human life to you?**

KEY WORDS

Sacred	Sanctity	Reincarnation
Abortion	Pro-Choice	Pro-Life
Sex	Chastity	Respect
Suicide	Euthanasia	Mishnah
Akirah	Agape	

4.1 IS LIFE SACRED?

In this lesson you will:
- investigate why some people believe that all life is sacred
- evaluate religious ideas about the sanctity and holiness of life
- give a personal response about whether life is sacred.

KEY WORDS

Sacred something of God or the divine

Sanctity purity or holiness

Reincarnation the belief that after death a person's soul moves into another body and continues to live

HOW SPECIAL IS LIFE?
HOW MUCH IS A LIFE WORTH?

Have you ever harmed an animal? Have you ever trodden on an insect, squashed a fly or washed a spider down the plug hole? How did you feel? Guilty? Sad? Nothing at all?

Have you ever held or seen a newborn child or animal? How did it make you feel?

How do you feel when you see a news report about a tragedy, for example earthquakes, wars or floods? Many people would admit to being deeply saddened when they see suffering in the world.

Some people believe that *all* life is **sacred** and should be respected. Some religious people argue this because they believe that life is God's creation. Some believe that humans and animals are all entitled to the right to life and should not be harmed.

In this lesson you will reflect on whether life is sacred. The proper term for this is 'the **sanctity** of life'.

🎧 **Have you ever held a newborn baby? How did it make you feel?**

Read through the following discussion between Molly and James:

Molly: I only eat free-range meat and eggs! I hate the idea of animals being cooped together with no space. It's so cruel!

James: Yeah! But at the end of the day you still eat the meat so you can't be that against it. If you thought all life was special, you'd be a vegetarian.

Molly: Not necessarily! It's okay to eat animals – that's what they're here for. But it's not okay to abuse them. We have a responsibility to care for them.

James: Well, I don't think we should worry about animals so much, when we can't even treat other humans with respect.

Molly: What do you mean?

James: Well, we go to war and kill people, and every day we hear about abortions, suicides and murders. We need to focus on getting humans to respect human life more first.

Molly: Hang on! There are some situations where it's okay to hurt other lives. What if someone invaded your country? You'd have to fight and kill people. Or what if you were 13 years old and became pregnant? You should be allowed to choose to have an abortion.

THINK ABOUT IT!

1. Add to this discussion. How might James respond to Molly's questions? What might he argue next?

● WHAT DO DIFFERENT RELIGIONS BELIEVE ABOUT THE SANCTITY OF LIFE?

As a Hindu I am against hurting any living thing. My religion teaches that all living things are special – plants, trees, and all creatures. The Hindu practice of worship includes respect for mountains and rivers as well as all living things. I follow the principle of ahimsa which means non-violence, and because of this I am a vegetarian. I also believe in **reincarnation** – the idea that after we die, we are reborn into a different form depending on how we lived in our previous life. The new form may be an animal, so I believe that it is important never to harm an insect or other living creature.

Maya

As a Christian I believe that all life is created by God and that the purpose of life is therefore to love and serve God. Animals are not equal to humans because only humans have souls and can go to heaven upon death. Many Christians don't have a problem with killing animals for meat. However, all life deserves respect, and God gave humanity the responsibility for looking after all creation, including animals and the environment – an idea called 'stewardship'. The Bible says that 'The Lord God took the man and put him in the Garden of Eden to work it and take care of it' (Genesis 2: 15). As a Christian I also believe that we have a responsibility to care for other people. The Bible gives us a 'golden rule' for this: 'Love God and love your neighbour as yourself' (Mark 12: 31).

Kim

THINK ABOUT IT!

2. Imagine that Maya and Kim join Molly and James in their discussion. Continue their discussion about the sanctity of life, to include both Christian and Hindu views.

3. **a)** How far do you agree with Maya's beliefs?
    b) How far do you agree with Kim's beliefs?

4. 'All life is sacred!' Do you agree? Write a few paragraphs to explain your views. You should include more than one point of view and some religious ideas in your answer.

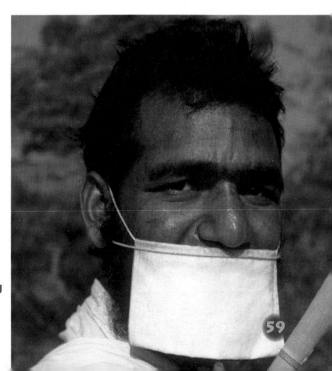

⤵ Jainism is a religion related to Hinduism. Jains believe that all life is sacred and show this by practising ahimsa. This Jain monk has his mouth covered so he does not accidently swallow and kill any insects.

In this lesson you will:
- investigate arguments for and against abortion
- evaluate whether abortion can ever be justified.

THINK ABOUT IT!

1. Look at the picture and its caption. They show a particular stage in the development of a human foetus.

   At what point do you think the foetus can be considered a human being? When it is an embryo? When it is a baby? When it can survive outside the womb? At birth?

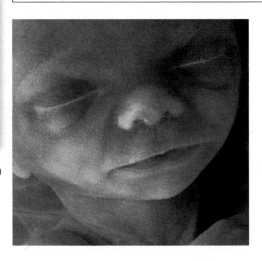

The embryo has become a foetus and is just over 5 cm (2 inches) long. Its vocal organs and sexual organs have formed. It is starting to suck and use the muscles it will later use in breathing.

The development of a human foetus:

Weeks 4–6	The embryo is the size of a poppy seed; its heart is a single tube with a few uncoordinated beats; bones begin to form.
Week 8	The embryo is about 2.5 cm long and makes slight movements; face developing, mouth starts to open.
Week 12	The embryo is a foetus just over 5 cm long. Its vocal organs and sexual organs have formed. It is starting to suck and use muscles it will later use to breath.
Week 20	The foetus is about 25 cm long. It kicks, twists, jumps and somersaults. Eyebrows and eyelashes start to form.
Week 28	The foetus is about 38 cm long and weighs just less than 1 kg. Its heartbeat speeds up when it hears its mother's voice. It could survive if born.
Week 40	The baby is ready to be born. It weighs about 4 kg and is about 55 cm long.

WHAT IS ABORTION?

An abortion is a medical procedure which removes the foetus from the womb prematurely (before it would naturally be born). In the UK, **abortions** are legal if the foetus is less than 24 weeks old and if two doctors consent to the abortion. Abortions are very common in the UK and it is now estimated that over 1 in 3 women will have at least one abortion in their lifetime.

In many countries around the world, however, abortion remains illegal – for example, in Ireland, Brazil and Egypt. And in many other countries, abortion is only legally permitted if the pregnancy poses a risk to the woman's physical or mental health, for example, in Australia, Portugal, Pakistan and Thailand.

WHY DO SOME PEOPLE THINK ABORTION IS ACCEPTABLE?

People who believe that the mother should have the freedom to choose whether or not to have an abortion are called 'Pro-Choice'.

Women's rights:
It is the mother's right to choose what happens to her own body. Having a baby is a huge, life-changing event and demands commitment.

PRO-CHOICE ARGUMENTS

Medical reasons:
Abortion might be the most humane option if the child will be born very ill or severely disabled.

It might be the fairest option for the mother/family because of the stress and upset caused by having and caring for such a seriously ill child.

Abortion should be an option when the pregnancy might damage the health of the mother.

Rape:
Abortion is morally acceptable if the pregnancy was caused by rape, because the child might be unwanted and might always remind the mother of that horrific event.

Social reasons:
The mother/family might not be able to afford to have a child.

Abortion should be an option for girls under 16 years old (the age of consent) because they might not be ready for motherhood, they may not have the support of their family, and having a child this young could 'limit' their future.

WHY ARE SOME PEOPLE AGAINST ABORTION?

People who are against abortion are often called **Pro-Life**.

Human rights:
Because each unborn baby has the potential to become a human being, it should have the same rights as any other human. The *UN Declaration of Rights of the Child* says that children are entitled to protection both before and after birth.

Adoption:
Thousands of people want to adopt a child and could give that child a loving and secure upbringing.

PRO-LIFE ARGUMENTS

Medical reasons:
Severely disabled children are unique humans and can lead very happy and fulfilling lives. Even if a child was born terminally ill, and only lived for a short time, it is better to live briefly than not at all.

Abortions are traumatic and can go wrong, causing damage to the mother.

THINK ABOUT IT!

2. Look at the above arguments for and against abortion.
   a) Choose two Pro-Choice reasons and write at least three sentences for each reason to explain why you agree or disagree with them.
   b) Now do the same for two Pro-Life reasons.

4.3 WHAT DO RELIGIOUS PEOPLE BELIEVE ABOUT SEX?

In this lesson you will:
- investigate what Christians and Buddhists believe about sex
- express your own views on sex and marriage.

THINK ABOUT IT!

1. Some people want to wait until they are married before they have sex. What do you think about this idea? Why might they want to wait? Discuss with your partner.

Some people wait until they are married before having sex.

WHAT IS SEX 'FOR'?

What is **sex** actually 'for'? This sounds like a silly question, but it is something that has been argued about for hundreds, if not thousands, of years by philosophers, psychologists, scientists and theologians. Look at some of the ideas below:

- Many people believe that sex is a biological way for reproducing new life – having children.
- Many people believe there is more to it than this.
- Some religious people, including many Muslims, Jews, Hindus, Sikhs and Christians, argue that sex is a gift from God, given so people can show love for their partner and become closer to them.

- Some scientists believe sex is a way of keeping a couple together so they can help raise their child together.
- Some people believe it is just a way of being able to have fun and that 'love' doesn't necessarily have to come into it.

THINK ABOUT IT!

2. Look at the ideas above. Which ones do you agree with? Which ones do you disagree with? Discuss with your partner, then feed back your ideas to the rest of the class.

WHAT DO CHRISTIANS BELIEVE ABOUT SEX?

Most Christians believe that sex is a gift from God that enables people to join together in an act of love and have children. Many Christians believe that sex should only be enjoyed in marriage because Jesus taught that it is wrong to have lustful thoughts. Because of this, many Christians believe that people should practise **chastity**, which means remaining a virgin until you are married.

> 'But I tell you that anyone who looks at a woman lustfully has already committed adultery with her in his heart'
>
> *The Bible, Mathew 5: 28*

However, some Christians believe it is acceptable to have sex outside marriage, as long as the couple love each other, are faithful to each other, and intend to have children.

Many Christians believe it is wrong to have extra-marital sex (to have an affair). This is because they believe marriage is sacred and is a union made before God. The seventh commandment in the Bible clearly states 'do not commit adultery' (Exodus 20: 14).

WHAT DO BUDDHISTS BELIEVE ABOUT SEX?

Buddhists do not believe in a creator god and they see marriage as a legal contract between people, rather than a divine gift. Because of this, most Buddhists believe it is acceptable to have sex before marriage. However, they also believe that sex should be approached with careful consideration. This is because sex can either lead to a healthier, happier way of life, or to unhappiness and suffering for yourself and others, depending on how you go about it.

Buddhists have a strict moral and ethical code part of which states they should abstain from sexual misconduct. Therefore, Buddhists think there are a number of things people should consider before sleeping with someone, to make sure the relationship is healthy and right for sex.

- Who are you going to have sex with and why? What are your motivations for having sex with this person?
- Sexual relationships should not be complicated. A person having an affair will need to lie about the fact that they are married, or lie to their partner about where they have been.
- Having sex with someone should not result in a guilty conscience. Sex should be an enjoyable experience for both people concerned.

Has the media changed people's attitudes towards sex?

THINK ABOUT IT!

3. Develop a leaflet or poster from a Buddhist or Christian point of view which puts forward that religion's ideas about appropriate sexual behaviour.

4. 'Sex should only happen within marriage.' Do you agree with this statement? Think of arguments both for and against this statement, and include some Christian and Buddhist ideas in your answer.

In this lesson you will:
- reflect on what it is like to grow older and how older people are treated
- investigate Muslim and Sikh views of older people
- express your own views on whether older people are shown the same respect as younger people.

KEY WORDS

Respect to feel or show admiration for something or someone you believe has good qualities

THINK ABOUT IT!

1. Look at the lyrics below. They are part of a song called 'Help the aged' by Pulp.

   Help the aged 'cos one day you'll be older too
   – you might need someone who can pull you through
   And if you look very hard behind the lines upon their face
   You may see where you are headed and it's such a lonely place.

   a) What different ideas does this song give about growing old?
   b) Do you agree with the messages of the song?

More than a third of older people experience loneliness.

THINK ABOUT IT!

2. How do these statistics make you feel? Do we treat older life with the same respect as younger life? Talk with your partner and prepare some comments to share with the class.

● IS OLDER LIFE TREATED WITH AS MUCH RESPECT AS YOUNGER LIFE?

As the lyrics above say, everyone will be elderly one day and might need help from other people in their lives. However, many older people today do not get the help, or **respect**, they need and deserve.

● WHAT IS IT LIKE TO BE OLDER?

With modern medical advances and improved standards of living, people are living much longer than they used to. Today, the over-60s are the fastest growing section of the world's population. The United Nations estimates that by the year 2025, 15 per cent of the population will be aged over 60 years, which is more than 1 in 7 people. Despite this, there are some very worrying facts about the care and treatment of the elderly in the UK:

- 630,000 people aged over 60 years have felt as though no-one knows they exist
- 7 out of 10 women and 4 in 10 men aged 85 or over live alone
- 1 in 6 older people have gone a whole week without speaking to anyone they know; 1 million older people will go a whole month
- 700,000 older people suffer from acute loneliness; 200,000 older people describe themselves as always feeling lonely.

HOW ARE OLDER PEOPLE TREATED IN ISLAM?

The idea of the 'family' is very important in Islam because the family is seen as the basic model of all society. Muslims are taught from a young age to treat older people in their family and the Muslim community with respect.

Muslims find the idea of sending older people into care homes or leaving them to live on their own as uncaring. They often prefer to live as extended families, with grandparents living in the same house or close to parents and children.

> 'Thy Lord has commanded that you...be kind to parents. Whether one or both of them attain old age in your lifetime, say not to them a word of contempt, nor repel them, but address them in terms of honour.'
>
> *Surah, 17:23*

HOW ARE OLDER PEOPLE TREATED IN SIKHISM?

There is a saying in India that 'old is gold', and this is certainly the Sikh view of the elderly. In Sikhism the family is very important and older people are seen as having a great role to play. Because they have lived through so much and have gained the most experience, the elderly are seen as the heads of the family and the key to passing on stories, history, culture and wisdom to the next generation.

As the heads of the family, older people are consulted in family matters and have the final say. The elderly perform important duties at special family events, such as birth ceremonies, weddings and funerals. Because of this, as in Islam, Sikhs often live as extended families.

THINK ABOUT IT!

3. **a)** Write a list of human rights that older people should have.
   b) Read through the way that Sikhs and Muslims treat elderly people. How do their actions match what you have included on your list?

4. 'Society would be better if more of us lived in extended families.' Do you agree? In your answer include arguments both for and against this statement.

Respect for older people is an important part of Sikhism.

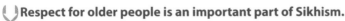
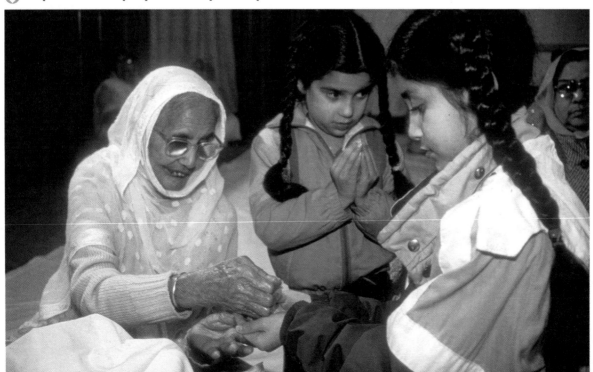

In this lesson you will:
- investigate euthanasia and how it affects people's lives
- explore religious and non-religious arguments for and against euthanasia
- evaluate whether it is ever right to help end someone's life.

KEY WORDS

Suicide the act of deliberately ending your own life

Euthanasia helping someone to painlessly end their own life

Mishnah a special ancient book of Jewish teachings and thoughts

Akirah Islamic belief in life after death

Dianne Pretty suffered from motor neurone disease. The disease can cause a slow and painful death.

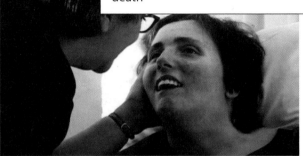

Terri Schiavo was severely brain damaged. She was incapable of controlled movement or communication with others. She was kept alive by a feeding tube.

Look at the pictures above and read the captions. Dianne Pretty wanted her husband to be able to help her commit **suicide** so that her suffering and pain could end. However, assisted suicide is against British law so Dianne took her case to court. She lost her case and died naturally on 12 May 2002.

Terri Schiavo died on 31 March 2005, fourteen days after doctors removed her feeding tube. Her husband wanted Terri to be allowed to die in this way but this was against the wishes of her parents, who had fought a seven-year legal battle to keep Terri alive.

THINK ABOUT IT!

1. Do you think Dianne Pretty's husband should have been allowed to help his wife die?

2. Do you think Terri Schiavo should have been allowed to live?

Write down your reactions and views or discuss them with a partner.

● WHAT IS EUTHANASIA?

Euthanasia is the term used for helping somebody to die in a painless way. It is usually performed on people with incurable and painful diseases and conditions. Although it is legal in some countries such as Holland and Switzerland, it is currently illegal in the UK.

There are two different *methods* of euthanasia:
- *Active* euthanasia means giving the person something that will painlessly end their life, such as a drug.
- *Passive* euthanasia means removing something that is needed to keep the person alive (such as a feeding tube or life-support machine).

There are two different *types* of euthanasia:
- 'Involuntary euthanasia' is performed without the person's permission, such as in the Terri Schiavo case when her feeding tube was withdrawn.
- 'Voluntary euthanasia' is euthanasia carried out at the request of the person killed – as Dianne Pretty had wanted. People assisting someone to die voluntarily risk being prosecuted for manslaughter or even murder.

a 'It is my life so I should have the right to be helped to die if I choose.'

b 'Where there is life there is hope.'

c 'People facing death might suffer from depression so they could be less able to make a rational decision about whether to end their life.'

d 'It is inhumane to allow people to suffer through terminal illness and incurable disease.'

e 'Pain-killing drugs can stop the suffering caused by illness.'

f 'New cures and treatments are being discovered all the time.'

g 'There are many cases of people making "miraculous" recoveries after being told they are expected to die.'

h 'Euthanasia makes human life worthless – it makes people disposable.'

i 'Euthanasia would ease the suffering of families and friends.'

j 'Euthanasia allows people to die peacefully, with dignity.'

k 'Accepting euthanasia will make it much easier for people facing death to cope with their own suffering.'

● WHAT DO MUSLIMS BELIEVE ABOUT EUTHANASIA?

Muslims believe that all life is sacred because it is created by Allah. To Muslims, euthanasia allows humans to choose their own ending and therefore to 'play God'. They believe that this is wrong because only Allah has the right to decide when a person should die. Muslims also believe that this life is a test of faith and that they will be judged before **Akirah**, the afterlife. Euthanasia interferes with Allah's plan and tests, so is never acceptable.

● WHAT DO JEWS BELIEVE ABOUT EUTHANASIA?

Judaism teaches that God is the creator and sustainer of all life. Therefore, nobody has the right to take human life except God. Jews believe that life is God's greatest gift and that saving and preserving human life should come before everything else. There is an important law in the Torah which says that Jews should set aside certain other religious laws in order to save a life. Because of this, euthanasia is not usually permitted in Judaism and a Rabbi would be consulted in each case.

THINK ABOUT IT!

3. Read through the list of arguments on this page. Decide which arguments are for euthanasia and which are against, then put them into two columns marked 'for' and 'against' in your books. Which side of the argument do you agree most with? Why?

4. There is an important Jewish teaching called **Mishnah** which says:
'Whoever destroys a single life is considered as if he had destroyed the whole world, and whoever saves a single life is considered as if he had saved the whole world.'
  a) Write down one question that you would like to ask about what this teaching means. Discuss your question in pairs.
  b) Do you agree with this teaching? Explain your ideas in detail.

4.6 DO PEOPLE HAVE THE RIGHT TO TAKE THEIR OWN LIFE?

In this lesson you will:
- investigate religious and non-religious attitudes towards suicide
- reflect on how people can support others thinking about ending their own life.

KEY WORDS

Agape Christian concept of unconditional love

🎧 **Kurt Cobain committed suicide in 1994. His suicide note said 'It's better to burn out than fade away'.**

Kurt Cobain was the lead singer of Nirvana, a grunge rock band that soared to fame in the early 1990s. He was a talented musician, a successful rock star and the father of a young child. On 5 March 1994, Cobain killed himself with a shotgun.

> 'There's good in all of us and I simply love people too much. So much that it makes me feel just too sad. Sad little sensitive unappreciated pieces.
>
> 'I had a good marriage, and for that I'm grateful...I'm pretty much of an erratic moody person, and I don't have the passion anymore. Peace, Love, Empathy, Kurt Cobain.'
>
> *Part of the suicide note Kurt Cobain left behind.*

? THINK ABOUT IT!

1. **a)** What do you think Kurt Cobain meant when he wrote 'It's better to burn out than fade away'?
   b) Kurt Cobain appeared to have everything going for him – a successful career, a family, fame and fortune. What factors might have caused this successful person to take his own life?

● HOW COMMON IS SUICIDE?

It is estimated that every 40 seconds somebody in the world commits suicide. In the UK, over 19,000 young people between the ages of 15 and 24 years attempt to commit suicide every year, resulting in over 700 deaths.

● WHY DO PEOPLE DECIDE TO TAKE THEIR OWN LIVES?

There are many causes of suicide, as the spider diagram below shows.

? THINK ABOUT IT!

2. What other factors would you add to the spider diagram? Write down your ideas.

3. Looking at these factors, how could you help change someone's mind who is considering taking his or her life? Discuss in pairs and write your ideas into your books.

Pressures from work — Loneliness — Loss of religious faith — Drink and drug problems — **Reasons why people commit suicide** — Relationship difficulties — Bullying — Money worries

The Samaritans is a charity which helps and counsels people thinking about suicide. Both religious and non-religious people volunteer to work for them and help others.

● WHAT DO CHRISTIANS BELIEVE ABOUT SUICIDE?

> 'In his hand is the life of every creature and the breath of all mankind.'
>
> *The Bible, Job 12: 10*

Christians believe that all life is sacred and ultimately belongs to God. Many Christians, therefore, believe that humans do not have the right to end their own lives and that suicide is a sin against God.

However, other Christians emphasize that God is loving and forgiving so would understand why people might choose to end their lives. They accept that people might commit suicide because they are emotionally unstable and not thinking clearly. Such Christians follow the teaching 'love God and love your neighbour as yourself' (Mark 12: 31) by trying to show suicidal people love and compassion. They believe that only by showing such love can humans create a caring community. The term for this unconditional love in Christianity is **agape**.

One way Christians might try to put agape into practice is to volunteer to work for charities such as 'The Samaritans'.

The Samaritans

The Samaritans began in 1953. A Church of England priest called Chad Varah discovered that three suicides were occurring every day in London. He put a telephone into his church so that anyone thinking of suicide could call him and he could listen to them and help.

Today the Samaritans have over 200 centres all around Britain and are involved in hospital, prison and school visits. The Samaritans is not a Christian charity – its volunteers come from all religions and many have no religion at all. There are over 22,000 volunteer workers in the organization, dedicated to helping people in distress. They act as an anonymous, caring voice at the end of the phone that will never judge, never preach about religion, but will just listen sympathetically and try to help.

THINK ABOUT IT!

4. What advice might a Christian give to someone thinking of taking their life? Write a paragraph to explain your ideas.

5. Design a poster to advertise jobs for volunteers for The Samaritans. It must explain the personal qualities needed by Samaritan volunteers, for example being a good listener.

In this lesson you will:
- reflect on the purposes of punishment
- investigate and evaluate the religious and non-religious arguments for and against capital punishment
- express your own beliefs about the use of capital punishment.

WHAT IS CAPITAL PUNISHMENT?

Capital punishment means paying for a crime with one's own life. It is also referred to as the 'death penalty' and the 'ultimate punishment', because it will be the final event of that person's life.

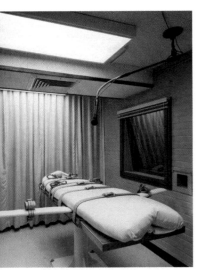

The last execution by hanging in the UK took place in August 1964. Capital punishment was abolished in the UK in 1965 for all crimes except treason and piracy. It was abolished entirely in 1998. This followed almost two hundred years of campaigning against the 'death penalty'.

In the USA today, 38 of its 50 states use capital punishment and most executions are carried out using lethal injection. Some Americans have argued that the USA should follow the UK's example.

A lethal injection chamber.

THINK ABOUT IT!

1. What is the point of punishment? Look at the list of possible reasons below:
   - to make society safer by removing known criminals
   - to get revenge on behalf of the victims of crime
   - to help the criminal become a positive member of society
   - to set an example to other would-be criminals
   - to make sure that society is fair – that bad actions are punished and good actions are rewarded.

   Which reason do you most agree with and which do you least agree with. Remember to explain your answers fully.

WHAT DOES CHRISTIANITY HAVE TO SAY ABOUT CAPITAL PUNISHMENT?

Some Christians have supported the use of capital punishment, commenting that the death sentence is an instruction found in the Old Testament.

However, other Christians have spoken out against capital punishment because it does not reflect their belief that human life is sacred – a special gift from God. They also point out that in the New Testament, Jesus speaks out against the use of violence for retaliation.

> '...eye for eye, tooth for tooth. As he has injured the other, so he is to be injured. Whoever kills an animal must make restitution; but whoever kills a man must be put to death.'
>
> *The Bible, Leviticus 24: 20–1*

> 'You have heard that it was said, "Eye for eye, and tooth for tooth." But I tell you, do not resist an evil person. If someone strikes you on the right cheek, turn to him the other also.'
>
> *The Bible, Matthew 5: 38–9*

● IS CAPITAL PUNISHMENT EVER THE ANSWER?

Below are some common arguments for and against the use of capital punishment.
There are many different and conflicting views surrounding this issue.

> Capital punishment is kinder than spending thirty years in prison.

> Capital punishment sets a bad example – it is never okay to kill a person.

> If you take away a person's life, you don't deserve to live.

> Sometimes people are proved innocent, years after they were sent to prison. How many innocent people have received the death penalty?

> Capital punishment doesn't work – some countries that have the death penalty also have higher crime rates than those that don't.

> Some people will always be a threat to society; capital punishment helps remove that threat.

> Capital punishment is not right. We should be able to forgive people who have committed crimes, not kill them.

?

◖ **Do you agree with these protesters?**

THINK ABOUT IT!

2. Prepare to enter the death penalty debate! The title of your debate is: 'Capital punishment can never be right.'
   a) You will need to write down:
      ● ideas that support this statement
      ● ideas that oppose this statement.
   b) When you have reached a decision about which side of the debate you will argue for, you will need:
      ● ideas, quotes and/or evidence in support of your argument
      ● ideas, quotes and/or evidence that highlight the problems of the opposite argument.

   Remember, your aim is to convince those listening that your opinion is right!

WHAT THE TASK IS ALL ABOUT:

- You are going to write a script for a TV talk-show debate between a number of religious people. They are going to be debating the statement:
'Humans should always protect and preserve life and never destroy it'.
- You must discuss and describe general religious ideas about the sanctity of life as well as religious views, using at least two of the following moral issues in your debate: abortion, euthanasia, sex and relationships, care of the elderly and capital punishment.
- The talk show will end with you, the presenter, giving your own views about the statement. You should also include your own views when discussing each of the religious topics.

WHAT YOU NEED TO DO TO COMPLETE THE TASK:

- The task is asking you to describe and explain different religious views about the sanctity of life. You should describe and explain religious views in as much detail as possible.
- You should include your own views throughout the discussions (remember to be respectful to the beliefs and ideas of others).
- You should finish by giving your own views about the statement 'Humans should always protect and preserve life and never destroy it'.

HINTS AND TIPS

- To do this task you could break down your script into 'mini-debates', focusing on some of the topics you have studied. For example, you could have a Muslim and a Jew discussing euthanasia and then include your own views as presenter. This could then be followed by a Christian and a Humanist discussing abortion.
- Include religious ideas you have studied in this chapter and your RE lessons.
- Remember that not all people from one religion will necessarily have the same views about a moral issue, for example Christians have different views about abortion. Try to show this in your script.

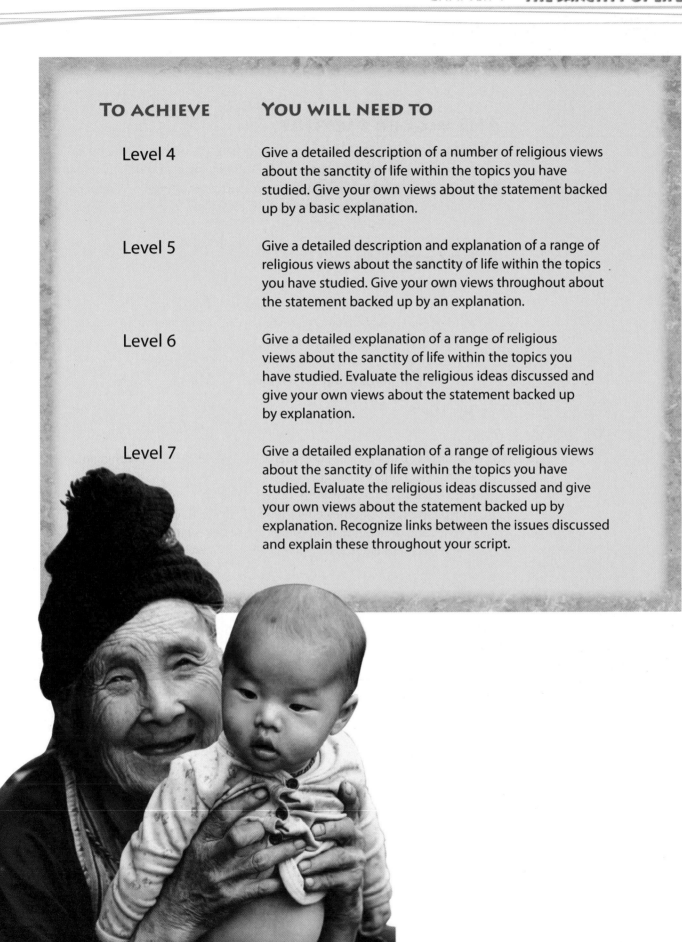

TO ACHIEVE	YOU WILL NEED TO
Level 4	Give a detailed description of a number of religious views about the sanctity of life within the topics you have studied. Give your own views about the statement backed up by a basic explanation.
Level 5	Give a detailed description and explanation of a range of religious views about the sanctity of life within the topics you have studied. Give your own views throughout about the statement backed up by an explanation.
Level 6	Give a detailed explanation of a range of religious views about the sanctity of life within the topics you have studied. Evaluate the religious ideas discussed and give your own views about the statement backed up by explanation.
Level 7	Give a detailed explanation of a range of religious views about the sanctity of life within the topics you have studied. Evaluate the religious ideas discussed and give your own views about the statement backed up by explanation. Recognize links between the issues discussed and explain these throughout your script.

5 INTERFAITH RELATIONSHIPS

THE BIGGER PICTURE

In this chapter you will be considering relationships within and between faith groups by looking at examples of interfaith collaboration and conflict. By studying these examples of agreement and disagreement you will begin to understand how religious people use their beliefs to make decisions.

WHAT?

You will:
- examine relationships between different faith groups
- interpret arguments and sources, explaining how they are used in different ways by different religious traditions
- analyse and evaluate the significance of collaborations and conflicts within and between religious faiths.

HOW?

By:
- studying examples of agreements and disagreements within and between religious groups
- comparing different arguments about key beliefs and issues, and expressing insight into how these affect the way that people live
- reflecting on a range of opinions about the relationships within and between religions.

WHY?

Because:
- religious belief has been the cause of some of the best but also some of the most harmful actions in the world
- some of the problems that affect people's lives today are the result of conflict between religions or world views
- if humanity had a better understanding of these problems and how they could be resolved, people would be more able to live in harmony with those whose beliefs differ.

🎧 **Members of different religious groups can achieve a great deal when they work together.**

KEY IDEAS

- The world contains many different religious groups. Many of the best and worst events in human history are the result of religious beliefs.
- There are also different beliefs and opinions within religious groups. We need to understand the ways in which religions interpret their scriptures and traditions in order to make sense of these differences.
- Sometimes religions are used to oppress people in ways which ignore the original religious teachings.
- We need to understand the conflicts and collaborations within and between different religious traditions in order to make sense of what goes on in the world and have a better chance of living in harmony with others.

KEY WORDS

Reconciliation	Dialogue
Injustice	Collaboration
Denominations	Gender
Non-Conformist	Ordained
Anglican Church	Apostle
Culture	Dowry
Hijab	Prejudice
Stereotype	Interfaith dialogue
Global ethic	

In this lesson you will:
- evaluate different causes of conflict
- reflect upon the role that religion has played in the conflicts within Northern Ireland
- investigate attempts to bridge conflict with collaboration.

KEY WORDS

Reconciliation putting aside past troubles

Dialogue communication, discussion of different viewpoints

Injustice unfairness

Collaboration working together to achieve a common goal

THINK ABOUT IT!

Below are nine issues that have contributed to troubles between different groups of people:

- clothing
- government
- language
- skin colour
- religion
- wealth
- postcode
- accent
- monarchy.

1. Read through the list and select the issue that you think would be:
   a) most likely to cause conflict
   b) most difficult to resolve
   c) easiest to resolve.
   Remember to explain your choices carefully.

● NORTHERN IRELAND – A HISTORY OF CONFLICT

The people of Northern Ireland have lived with conflict over a period of nearly 500 years. In 1534 Henry VIII, then King of England and Ireland, established a Protestant Church and broke away from the Roman Catholic Church. However, many of the people of Ireland wanted to remain Catholic and resented these new changes.

Disputes continued over hundreds of years and then in 1921 the British government imposed a geographical split in Ireland between the mainly Protestant north-east and the Catholic south. This created the state of Northern Ireland and led to further political disputes. Over the following years, Catholics and Protestants in Northern Ireland continued to be divided in terms of religion, politics and geography. By the end of the 1960s, relationships between many Catholics and Protestants were marked by extreme violence on both sides. Catholics in Northern Ireland campaigned for equality in housing, employment, education and politics.

⏱ **The aftermath of a civil rights protest in Londonderry, 1969.**

THINK ABOUT IT!

2. Look closely at the picture of the aftermath of the disputes between Protestants and Catholics in Northern Ireland. How do you think people would have felt living in Northern Ireland during this time? Who or what do you think people would have blamed for the troubles?

● CORRYMEELA – A CHANCE FOR HARMONY

In 1965 a group of Christians in Northern Ireland formed a new Christian community that could act as a bridge between Catholics and Protestants. This community is known as Corrymeela, meaning 'harmony hill'.

Since it started, Corrymeela has been dedicated to helping Protestants and Catholics live peacefully alongside one another. In order to achieve this goal the community has run and funded many different projects that give Catholics and Protestants the chance to meet and discuss their differences and similarities in safe environments. Below are the aims and objectives of Corrymeela.

The Revd Ray Davey, the founder of Corrymeela.

Corrymeela – aims and objectives

- To be a sign and symbol that Protestants and Catholics can share together in a common witness and ministry of **reconciliation**.

- To provide opportunities for meeting, **dialogue** and learning in communities to dispel ignorance, prejudice and fear and to promote mutual respect, trust and co-operation.

- To support victims of violence and **injustice**; to enable the healing of personal and social wounds and to promote new initiatives for social and political change.

- To address contemporary issues of faith and ethics and develop new expressions of Christian community, life and worship.

The following spider diagram shows the different **collaboration** projects undertaken at Corrymeela.

Open meetings for all religious traditions on social, cultural, political and religious themes.

Events, such as festivals, that allow Catholics and Protestants to meet in a peaceful environment.

Corrymeela – collaboration projects

Opportunities for Catholic and Protestant students to meet and ask questions of each other.

Supporting students in Catholic and Protestant schools to work with each other on a variety of projects.

THINK ABOUT IT!

3. Look at the aims and objectives of Corrymeela and the collaboration projects that it runs.
   a) How well do you think these are linked?
   b) Suggest some other projects that Corrymeela could run. How would they be linked to the aims and objectives?

4. What reasons can you think of for focusing collaboration projects on schools?

In this lesson you will:
- investigate some of the major arguments within Christianity about whether women should have positions of authority in the Church
- analyse ways in which denominations of Christianity interpret questions of authority in different ways.

KEY WORDS

Denominations different branches of the Christian Church

Gender being male or female

Non-conformist Christain denominations which broke away from the Church of England

Ordained having a special service to become a priest or minister

Anglican Church the body of churches around the world that are in communion with the Church of England

WHAT IS THE ROLE OF WOMEN WITHIN CHRISTIANITY?

In Christianity there has been much discussion about whether women can hold positions of authority in the Church. The Christian Church across the world is made up of many **denominations**. The largest denomination, the Roman Catholic Church, teaches that women should not become priests. In the Roman Catholic Church it is believed that the Pope is important because he is in a direct line from St Peter who was given his authority from Jesus.

> 'You are Peter and on this rock I shall build my church.'
>
> *Matthew 16:18*

The second largest Christian denomination, the Orthodox Church, also holds this view.

The Roman Catholic Church has great respect for Mary, the mother of Jesus. Her humble acceptance of God's purpose for her is seen as an example for women to follow.

As Roman Catholics we believe that women have an important role to play, especially in the family, but scripture and the example of Jesus show that they should not be leaders in the Church. According to the Christian scriptures, all Jesus' disciples were men. This proves that women should not be ordained as priests.

Kim

I belong to the Society of Friends, usually known as the Quakers. A central belief for the Quakers is that there is a part of God's spirit in every human soul. This means that all people, regardless of their **gender**, have the same importance. For this reason women and men are both leaders in our community.

George

Margaret Fell, a female leader in the Quakers, wrote a pamphlet in 1660 to argue that equal roles for men and women was in keeping with God's teaching.

? THINK ABOUT IT!

1. Read Luke 1: 26–35. In what ways could the Virgin Mary be a role model for women in the Catholic Church?

WOMEN AS EQUALS

In some other Christian denominations, however, women hold equal authority with men. The Society of Friends, usually known as the Quakers, began in Britain in the 1650s and takes a different view.

The Quakers broke away from the Church of England to form a separate Christian community because they disagreed with its teachings and organization. For this reason the Quakers are known as a **Non-conformist** denomination. Quakers do not agree with the priesthood so they choose ministers or elders to lead them instead. Because they refused to accept the authority of the established church many of the Quakers were punished and imprisoned for their beliefs. Important leaders in the beginning of Quakerism were George Fox and his wife, Margaret Fell. They believed they had been contacted directly by God and that everyone had the 'spark of God' within them. Margaret Fell preached at meetings, wrote pamphlets about Quaker beliefs and gave help, support and advice to travelling Quaker preachers.

Other non-conformist denominations include Methodist, Baptist, and Pentecostal Churches and the Salvation Army. These have ministers who are **ordained**. Antoinette Brown was the first woman to be ordained as a minister in a non-conformist church called the Congregational Church in 1853. Many people disagreed with her ordination, however, and she eventually had to leave the Church. The Methodist Church began to ordain women ministers in 1880.

Of the churches which have priests, only the **Anglican Church** has ordained women and there has been a great deal of disagreement about this within the Church of England.

🎧 **This Anglican priest is blessing the bread and wine in the central Christian service of Eucharist. Not all Christians agree that women should be able to have such authority.**

THINK ABOUT IT!

2. Produce a mind map showing how the Roman Catholic Church and Quakerism have different beliefs about authority from God and the role of women.

3. Why do you think that non-conformist churches ordained women long before churches with priests and bishops?

In this lesson you will:
- examine the ways in which Christians use their scriptures and teachings to decide on the place of women in the church
- discuss and evaluate the arguments presented by Christians in debates about the place of women in the church.

KEY WORDS

Apostle disciples 'sent out' by Jesus

Debates about the place of women in a faith community can highlight the different ways in which people within that religion understand their scriptures and tradition. This can be illustrated by Christian opinions about whether or not women should be priests.

In 1992 the first female priests were ordained into the Church of England.

WHY ARE THERE DIFFERENCES IN BELIEFS?

Christians who agree with women priests often interpret the Bible differently from those who say that women cannot have authority in the Church.

'The Bible includes the teachings of many people over many centuries. We might believe that all these writers were inspired by God, but they could only express God's word in the ideas of their own time and culture. As a result, there are some differences in the Bible and Christians have to decide which teachings are closest to what God wants.'

Some of the first 32 women to be ordained into the Anglican Church.

● TEACHINGS THAT SUPPORT WOMEN HAVING EQUALITY WITH MEN

When looking at the creation story in the Old Testament (Genesis 2: 4–24), some scholars argue that in Hebrew, the original language of the Bible, 'Adam' means 'human' and not 'male'. So male and female would be made from the first 'human'. This agrees with the other creation account in Genesis (1: 27).

In the Christian scriptures of the New Testament, some teachings indicate that women should have equality with men.

> 'There is neither Jew nor Greek, there is neither slave nor free, there is neither male nor female; for all are one in Christ Jesus.'
>
> *The Bible, Galatians, 3: 28*

> 'So God created man in his own image...male and female he created them.'
>
> *The Bible, Genesis 1: 27*

> 'There are "clues" in the Gospels that Jesus treated women as equal in authority to men, but that these have been lost in the way that the Bible has been put together. For instance, the Gospels tell that Mary Magdalene was the first person to see Jesus after the resurrection and was given the instruction to tell the other disciples. (Matthew 28: 1–7; Mark 16: 1–7; Luke 24: 1–12; John 20: 11–18). This can be interpreted to mean that she was an **apostle** yet the major Churches teach that women cannot be priests because they were not apostles.'

● TEACHINGS THAT DISAGREE WITH WOMEN HAVING EQUALITY WITH MEN IN THE CHURCH

However, in the New Testament there are also teachings against women being leaders in the Christian Church.

Some Christians argue that the creation story in Genesis shows that women should not have authority over men because Adam was created before Eve. Some Christians go further and say that the Bible was written down and translated by people whose ideas were influenced by the society of their time, in which women were considered inferior to men.

> 'I do not permit a woman to teach or to have authority over a man; she must be silent. For Adam was formed first, then Eve.'
>
> *The Bible, 1 Timothy, 2: 12–13*

THINK ABOUT IT!

1. Imagine that you are a Christian debating whether women should be allowed to be priests. (This might require you to empathize with a position other than your own.) Use the information in this lesson to list as many arguments as possible on both sides of the debate. Remember, if you were a Christian, the teachings of the Bible and of the Church would be important to you.

Here are some more Bible passages for you to consider in your arguments:
- 1 Corinthians 14: 33–6
- Ephesians 5: 21–4

2. Using your lists, decide which side of the debate you agree with most. Now write your speech either agreeing or disagreeing with whether women should be allowed to become priests.

In this lesson you will:
- examine the debates around the place of women in Sikhism
- investigate the different ways in which religions use their sources and teachings
- explore the impact of Sikh beliefs about women in the world today.

KEY WORDS

Culture a way of life based on the customs of a particular time or place

Dowry an amount of money which has to be paid to the family of a woman's husband when she gets married

WOMEN'S EQUALITY IN SIKHISM

Equality is at the very heart of Sikhism's teaching. The Gurus, who brought God's words to Sikhism, criticized the society of their day for its unfair treatment of women and spoke out against some of the practices that existed at the time. These practices included killing babies because they were female and expecting women to commit suicide on their husband's death by throwing themselves on the funeral pyre (the fire for burning the dead body).

The Gurus taught that women could take part in every aspect of Sikh life and worship because they were of equal importance to men. This is stated clearly in the Sikh holy scriptures.

Although all the Gurus were men, women played an important part in the history of Sikhism. Bibi Nanaki was the elder sister of Guru Nanak who he regarded as his inspiration and mentor. Nanaki was the first person to be initiated into Sikhism by Guru Nanak and she encouraged her brother in his life's work.

During the guruship of Guru Amar Das, 52 female missionaries helped to spread the teaching of Sikhism.

THINK ABOUT IT!

1. Set up a debate for and against the statement 'Sikhism does not show equality to women because all the Gurus were men'.

All Sikhs are expected to marry but the Gurus taught that marriage must be seen as a relationship of two equal partners. Guru Amar Das described this as 'one spirit in two bodies'. A Sikh woman keeps her own name after marriage and does not have to change it to her husband's.

The scriptures also use language to show that God is neither male nor female. In its original language, the Guru Granth Sahib is written without gender, meaning that it does not use male or female terms. (When it is translated into English, however, God is usually referred to as 'he'.) Some of the most important prayers in Sikhism refer to God as father and mother.

RELIGION AND CULTURE

The Sikh Gurus introduced customs which showed that women had equal standing in marriage. For instance, even when they are married, Sikh women keep their own name – Kaur, meaning 'princess'. However, some Sikh women complain that in several Sikh communities, women are not allowed the freedom and authority that the Gurus taught. They argue that the long-held customs of some societies, in which women are understood to be inferior to men, have greater influence than the teachings of Sikhism. A way of life, based on such customs, is referred to as a person's **culture**.

I have been brought up in a Sikh family where I am treated as an equal. I am very proud of my Sikh identity. Yet my family tell me that when I was born, distant relatives sent my parents blessings that sounded more like sympathies than congratulations. Apparently, they pitied them for the **dowry** they would have to pay. They mentioned the inheritance I could never receive, and the family name that could never survive by me. One can imagine their joy and relief upon my brother's birth two years later. I just can't understand how Sikhs could still hold ideas like this 500 years after Guru Nanak taught about equality! At least I have the teachings of my religion to argue against them.

Ranjit

THINK ABOUT IT!

2. Why do you think this woman's relatives still thought of women as inferior to men despite the fact that they were Sikhs? How can Sikh women use the teachings of their religion to argue against the unfair treatment of women?

This is how one female Sikh writer has described the problem of women's role in Sikh culture.

'The Sikh community needs to look beyond the ingrained customs and know the true nature of justice and equality; the Sikh community needs to realise its entanglement in a system that accepts practices which go against the very basis of the Sikh faith, against the very word of God. The Sikh community needs to shake itself to awaken and rise into a truly strong and powerful religious people, living the way God desires us to live: by freedom, justice, love, and equality – for all.'

Women and men both have the same religious duties.

THINK ABOUT IT!

3. What do you think the writer of the above quote means by 'ingrained customs'?

4. What questions would you like to ask the writer?

5.5 HIJAB – A CASE STUDY

In this lesson you will:
- examine the teachings in Islam about correct dress for Muslims
- investigate the debates around the wearing of hijab
- communicate the arguments for and against the view that Muslim women are oppressed by wearing the hijab.

KEY WORDS

Hijab a head covering used by Muslim women

There is a great deal of misunderstanding about Islam. One accusation that some non-Muslims make against Islam is that it is unfair to women. There are many opinions about whether Muslim women should wear **hijab** or 'the veil'. In this lesson you will explore these views as part of a case study of debates about women in religion, because they provide a good example of the key issues.

WHY DO SOME MUSLIM WOMEN CHOOSE TO WEAR HIJAB?

Islam teaches that women and men should dress modestly. Some of the most important teachings about this in the Qur'an are shown below.

> 'Say to believing men that they should lower their gaze and guard their modesty; ...And say to the believing women that they should lower their gaze and guard their modesty; and that they should not display their beauty and ornaments except what must ordinarily appear; that they should draw their veils over their bosoms and not display their beauty except to their close male relatives ...'
>
> *Qur'an 24: 30–1*

> 'Believing women should cast their outer garments over themselves (when outside); this is most convenient, that they should be recognized (as Muslims) and not be molested.'
>
> *Qur'an 33: 59*

🎧 **In some Muslim countries, women are expected to cover themselves completely when they are in public.**

Modest and respectful behaviour between men and women is an important part of Muslim teaching. How this affects what is worn is interpreted in different ways by different Muslim women and in different Muslim cultures.

Most Muslim women wear loose-fitting clothes which hide most of their body and headscarves to cover their hair. This head covering is called **hijab**. Some non-Muslims think that women are made to dress like this because they are oppressed, meaning that they are treated as inferior and are controlled by men.

Many Muslim women disagree with this and point out that they choose to wear hijab. For them, the wearing of hijab is important to their identity as Muslims and does not prevent them from playing an active part in public life. Some Muslim women have campaigned for the right to wear traditional Muslim dress when others have tried to stop them.

A good example of this is the recent protest by Muslim girls against the ban on wearing hijab in French schools. There is a law in France that religion must not be taught in public schools and, as a part of this law, it was decided in 2004 that religious symbols would also be banned. This ban included large Christian crucifixes, Jewish skullcaps, Sikh turbans and the Muslim hijab. Many Muslim girls have protested against this law and dozens have chosen to defy the rule and be expelled from school rather than give up something they believe in.

In some countries women have campaigned for their right to wear hijab.

‘We want to stop men from treating us like sex objects, as they have always done. We want them to ignore our appearance and to take notice of our personalities and mind. We want them to take us seriously and treat us as equals and not just chase us around for our bodies and physical looks.’

An Iranian Muslim schoolgirl's views on the French ban of wearing hijab to school.

THINK ABOUT IT!

1. Explain, in your own words, how the Muslim schoolgirl speaking above argues that hijab gives her freedom and respect.

THINK ABOUT IT!

2. Imagine that you are a Muslim teenager. Write a letter to your school or an article for the school magazine, explaining why you believe Muslim girls should be allowed to wear hijab to school.

3. Some Muslim women choose not to wear hijab. What arguments might they use to show that they do not need to cover their heads. Look carefully at the rights given to women in Islam to help you answer this question.

It is possible to question whether Western non-Muslim women really 'choose' the way they dress or whether they are persuaded to do so by the pressures of advertising and what other people expect. Some Muslim women would argue that the pictures of half-naked women used for advertising and entertainment show that Western culture does not respect women.

In some Muslim countries, women are mistreated, but this is because the teachings of Islam are being ignored or religion is used as an excuse to oppress women.

Muslims point out that when Islam began as an organized religion, many of the first converts were women because it gave them new rights and freedoms. In the time of Prophet Muhammad, women like Kadijah, his first wife, Ayesha, his later wife, and Fatima, his daughter, were recognized as having authority and wisdom in the community. Also, the Qur'an makes it clear that women should be educated and should never be forced to marry against their will. In Islam, women have always been able to keep their own wealth and property in marriage, rights that British women didn't have until the nineteenth century.

In this lesson you will:
- investigate the causes and effects of Islamophobia
- reflect on and challenge your own opinions and how you have formed them.

KEY WORDS

Prejudice believing some people are inferior or superior without even knowing them

Stereotype a fixed, unchanged idea about a person or group of people, usually based on prejudice

THINK ABOUT IT!

1. At some point in our lives we are all treated unfairly.
   a) Use the sentence starters below to write about an example of unfair treatment that you have experienced.
      - I was treated unfairly when...
      - This made me feel...because...
      - I reacted by...
      - I think this was effective/ineffective because...
   b) Think carefully about how you reacted to the unfair treatment you received. Would you react differently if it occurred now? If yes, how would you act differently?

● WHAT ARE THE EFFECTS OF ISLAMOPHOBIA?

Islamophobia is an unreasonable fear or hatred of Muslims based on their faith and religious background. It is a form of **prejudice** that is often based upon **stereotypes** of Muslims and misunderstandings about the Islamic faith. In recent years, Muslims have reported being physically and verbally abused because of their religion.

⊓ **Sabeel is a Muslim teenager in the UK.**

Sometimes, people who don't know me are shocked when I tell them I'm a Muslim, and they treat me a bit differently. Some people act scared. I think some people just repeat the things they hear without thinking but it is frustrating because for me and for many Muslims, Islam is a religion that brings peace through getting to know God; it is not something to be afraid of.

🎧 **Sabeel's experiences of being a Muslim in the UK.**

THINK ABOUT IT!

2. a) How do you think Sabeel is made to feel by Islamophobia?
   b) What advice would you give to him? Remember to reflect upon your own experiences of unfair treatment.

● DOING SOMETHING ABOUT IT!

Some people have suggested that Islamophobia is difficult to challenge because it is the product of many different, smaller ideas. For example, the way that Muslims are reported in the news; do we hear about Muslims in a positive light, such as being involved in charity work or in a negative light, such as being involved in conflict? However, if we challenge how reliable these ideas are, it is possible to do something to prevent this spread of ignorance and fear.

We often react to other people based on the ideas that we have about them. But how often do we stop to think where our ideas come from? For example, how is our thinking influenced by the ideas of our friends or family, or by what we see?

THINK ABOUT IT!

3. What influences your ideas about others? Where do 'your' opinions come from?

   a) Create a spider diagram to show 'My influences'. Arrange the diagram so that the bigger the influence, the closer it is to the centre. An example is shown below.

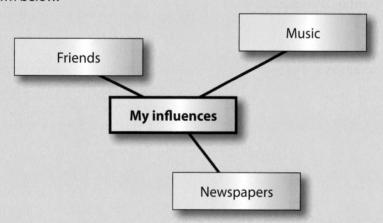

   b) Next to each of your influences, add the amount of time you spend with that person/on that activity each week.

   ● Does the amount of time you spend affect how important the influence is?

   ● Are there any influences that you might bring closer to the centre or move further away based on how much time you spend on them?

4. After you have completed the activity above, answer the following questions:

   a) How do I treat others?

   b) How do I want to be treated by others?

   c) Why do I treat some people better than others?

   d) Do other people tell me what to think? If so, who?

   e) Who or what is my biggest influence?

   f) Are the people who influence me reliable?

In this lesson you will:
- examine ways in which religions have worked together to build interfaith dialogue
- investigate the ways in which religions collaborate to address problems in the world
- evaluate whether interfaith dialogue can have an effect on global problems.

KEY WORDS

Interfaith dialogue discussions and work carried out between different faiths

Global ethic a code of conduct for the whole world

A WORLD OF DIFFERENCE

There are many religions and faith communities in the world, all with different beliefs about God, humans and the world. In the past few years there have been several occasions when representatives of many of the world's religions have met together to talk about what they have in common, how they can work together, and discuss where they differ. This is referred to as **interfaith dialogue**.

THINK ABOUT IT!

1. Using the ideas you have been given in this book, and your own ideas, list as much evidence as you can to support the view that:
   a) disagreements within and between religions have caused much unhappiness in the world
   b) ethical teachings and spirituality in religions can help people to make the world a better place.

RELIGIONS WORKING TOGETHER FOR A BETTER WORLD

After the terrorist attack on the World Trade Centre in New York on 11 September 2001, more than 200 religious leaders from many different faiths came together for a Day of Prayer for Peace in Assisi, Italy. Until that day, religious leaders of all denominations had never participated in the same prayer meeting. They wanted to show that religions should not use violence against one another but work together for a better world. The meeting finished with a joint commitment to peace.

'Violence never again! War never again! Terrorism never again! In the name of God, may every religion bring upon the Earth justice and peace, forgiveness and life, love!'

Joint commitment to peace arising from the Day of Prayer for Peace, 24 January 2002

PARLIAMENT OF THE WORLD'S RELIGIONS

In 1993, an even larger gathering of faiths was held in Chicago, USA, to celebrate the centenary (100 years) of the Parliament of the World's Religions. The original meeting in 1893 was the first major interfaith conference in recorded history. It brought together eastern and western spiritual leaders to learn from and with each other. The Parliament of the World's Religions has since met again, in South Africa in 1999, and in Spain in 2004.

'The mission of the Council for a Parliament of the World's Religions is to cultivate harmony between the world's religious and spiritual communities and foster their engagement with the world and its other guiding institutions in order to achieve a peaceful, just, and sustainable world.'

How the group which organizes the Parliament's meetings explained its mission.

THINK ABOUT IT!

2. **a)** Write out the Parliament's mission, which means intention or purpose, in your own words.
   b) What is the Parliament of the World's Religions trying to do?

In the meetings of the Parliament of the World's Religions, people from many different faiths, including Paganism and Native American religions, gather together to discuss, debate, worship and learn from one another. One of the most important purposes of the Parliament is to show how religious believers can work together to make the world a better place. This is called a **global ethic**. Below are some extracts from the Parliament of the World's Religions' *Declaration Toward a Global Ethic*, written in 1993.

🎧 **The Parliament of World Religions is a good example of interfaith dialogue. In 2004 it met in Barcelona, Spain.**

'We must treat others as we wish others to treat us. We make a commitment to respect life and dignity, individuality and diversity, so that every person is treated humanely, without exception. We must have patience and acceptance. We must be able to forgive, learning from the past but never allowing ourselves to be enslaved by memories of hate. Opening our hearts to one another, we must sink our narrow differences for the cause of the world community, practising a culture of solidarity and relatedness...

'Therefore, we commit ourselves to this global ethic, to understanding one another, and to socially beneficial, peace-fostering, and nature-friendly ways of life.

'We invite all people, whether religious or not, to do the same.'

Extracts from the Parliament of the World's Religions' Declaration Toward a Global Ethic, 1993

THINK ABOUT IT!

3. Do you think it is a good idea to develop a 'global ethic'? Give reasons for your answer, using language from the declaration.

4. Do you think that religions might have a better chance to influence world leaders than other organizations? What sort of influence might they have?

WHAT THIS TASK IS ALL ABOUT:

1. 'Religions cause more harm than good!' Do you agree?
Give reasons for your answer, showing that you have considered both sides of the argument. Use religious examples and teachings to support your answer.

In this chapter you have studied some examples of the relationships within and between different faiths. You have explored the issues arising from these inter-faith relationships and how such issues are seen and addressed. For many people, religion and faith are a great source of strength and inspiration; however, it has often been said that religion is the cause of most of the world's problems.

This task asks you to give your opinion on this debate. You need to explain the reasons for your opinions and show that you have considered the debate from both sides. You also need to use teachings and examples from religions to support the points that you make.

WHAT YOU NEED TO DO TO COMPLETE THE TASK:

- Start by considering the reasons that people might have for agreeing with the view that 'Religions cause more harm than good!', and the reasons that they might have to disagree with it. It may help you to create two separate lists of reasons: one for and one against.
- Next, decide which side of the debate you are most convinced by, and what the most convincing reason is. You can remain undecided, but you must be prepared to give good reasons for your view nevertheless to explain why you have found it hard to choose one side or the other.
- You will then have to select some key examples from the religions that you have looked at in this chapter and use them as evidence that helps to explain the views on both sides of the argument as well as in support of your own view. Remember to clearly explain where each of the key examples comes from, what it means and how it can be used in this argument.

HINTS AND TIPS

Remember, your own point of view is very important here. Be careful to support your viewpoint by fully explaining it and referring to religious examples and teachings. You must also remember that the key to this task is balance – you must put forward *both* sides of the argument, both for and against the key statement.

TO ACHIEVE	YOU WILL NEED TO
Level 4	Show understanding of some of the reasons for agreeing and disagreeing with the key statement. Show how these ideas are put into use in religious examples and/or teachings.
Level 5	Explain a selection of the reasons for agreeing and disagreeing with the key statement, including your own viewpoint. Explain how religious examples and/or teachings might be used to support agreeing or disagreeing with the key statement.
Level 6	Explain the reasons why people might agree and disagree with the key statement. Give and explain your own viewpoint, using examples and teachings from religion(s).
Level 7	Using subject key words confidently, explain in detail the reasons for agreeing and disagreeing with the key statement. Show that you have weighed up the different arguments and explain how they fit with your own viewpoint.

ARE THERE MORE QUESTIONS THAN ANSWERS?

THE BIGGER PICTURE

In this chapter you will be thinking back to some of the topics you have studied in RE over the last three years and identifying some of the questions they have raised for you. During the past three years you may have considered whether it is the human ability to ask and (attempt to) answer complex questions that makes humanity unique. Here you will be asking questions about questions!

● Do all questions have answers?
● What questions do you find most puzzling?
● Do the different religions and life stances you have studied have the answers?
● Is it alright to keep asking questions even when there seem to be no answers?

WHAT?

You will:

● explore in depth some of the 'big questions' about life and death, and what it means to be human
● ask your own questions
● interpret and evaluate the different ways in which people try to understand the world
● reflect on your own responses to these questions.

HOW?

By:

● discussing questions in depth and suggesting your own ideas about how they might be answered
● investigating different responses, both religious and secular, to ultimate questions
● using reasoning to make an informed account of other people's beliefs and ideas
● asking 'why?' and 'why not?'
● thinking deeply about the questions and your own responses to them.

WHY?

Because:

● everyone, whether they are religious or not, has questions they would like to ask about the meaning and purpose of life
● the answers which people give to such questions often impact on the way they behave
● analysing the beliefs, ideas and uncertainties of others will help you to understand why people do what they do.

KEY IDEAS

- Asking and trying to answer complex religious and philosophical questions about the meaning and purpose of life is a uniquely human characteristic.
- Thinking about the questions posed by others and how they have tried to answer them helps us to understand how others see the world.
- There are more questions than answers.
- Some people think they have the 'right' answers to ultimate questions.

KEY WORDS

Ultimate questions	Philosopher
Theologian	Secular
Mystic	Metaphor
Envoy	Resurrection
Contempt	Arrogance
Dogma	Ghetto
Dilemma	Moral dilemma
Innocence	Utilitarianism
Visionary	Justice
Conflict resolution	

⟨ **Are there more questions than answers?**

In this lesson you will:

- ask and answer questions that you find puzzling about your own experience and the feelings of others
- explore the different approaches of philosophy and theology to answering questions
- use theological and philosophical language to raise and suggest answers to a range of questions
- reflect on and express your own responses to some of the questions posed in this lesson.

KEY WORDS

Ultimate questions questions about the meaning and purpose of life, death and the place of humans in the universe

Philosopher someone who thinks deeply and asks questions to try and understand the meaning of life

Theologian someone who thinks about questions raised by and about religions

Secular a non-religious way of life or thinking

● WHAT ARE 'ULTIMATE QUESTIONS'?

Ultimate questions are questions about the meaning and purpose of life and death, and what it means to be human.

A group of people each wrote down the one question they find the most puzzling about life, to which they would really like to know the answer. Their responses are shown in the speech bubbles below.

> Why do humans question things? (Carolynne, 40)

> Who made the world? (Laurie, 11)

> What is electricity? (Hal, 8)

> What's the meaning of life? (Eleanor, 10)

> What's the point of questioning? (Ashraf, 33)

> Is there life after death? (Alfie, 15)

Can questions like these be answered – and, if so, how we might go about finding those answers? If they can be answered, what answers can be given? And how would we know whether such answers are right or not? Two approaches to exploring questions like these are through philosophy and theology.

● WHAT IS PHILOSOPHY?

> In philosophy you can ask questions you've always wanted to ask about things you've always wanted to know. (Anna, Year 6 student)

> Philosophy begins in wonder. (Alfred North Whitehead, philosopher)

THINK ABOUT IT!

1. Write down the most puzzling 'ultimate question' you can think of on a sticky note. Display all the questions posed by your class so that you can come back to them later.

Philosophy is not like science or maths. It doesn't rely on formal means of proof, such as experiments and observations. It relies entirely on thought. Philosophy is done by asking questions and debating, trying out ideas and thinking of possible arguments against them.

Socrates (469–399 BC) was a Greek **philosopher** who lived in Athens. He showed that life could be focused on asking the 'why, what and which questions' that interest, puzzle or make people curious. The point of Socratic dialogue is to ask questions in order to discover the truth. The truth can only be found by people who are prepared to listen and think as well as talk, and who are open to new ideas.

● WHAT IS THEOLOGY?

'Theology is thinking about questions raised by and about the religions...it is a subject which deals with questions of meaning, truth, beauty and practice raised in relation to religions.'

David F. Ford, **theologian**

Theology (a Greek word which literally means 'word of God') tackles ultimate questions from the viewpoint that there is a powerful force or being outside human existence. Theology cannot be **secular** so theological answers to ultimate questions will draw on religious beliefs.

Hans Kung, a Christian theologian, created a list of ultimate questions, which are shown below. We will continue to look at some possible answers to some of these 'Big Questions'.

There is a story about a theologian and a philosopher who blunder around in a dark room looking for a cat that isn't there. The theologian finds the cat!

What can we know?
Why is there anything at all, why not nothing?
Where do we come from and where do we go to?
Why is the world as it is?
What is the ultimate reason and meaning of all reality?
What ought we to do?
Why, and when, are we finally responsible?
What do we despise and what do we value?
What is the point of loyalty and friendship, but also what is the point of suffering and sin?
What really matters for humanity?
What may we hope?
Why are we here?
What is it all about?
What is there left for us, death making everything pointless at the end?
What will give us courage for life, and what courage for death?

Adapted from On being a Christian *by Hans Küng, theologian*

THINK ABOUT IT!

2. Philosophers and theologians: what's the difference? Explore this question through the cartoon above, using a community of enquiry. Some questions you might ask about the story are:
   ● What does it mean?
   ● Does it mean that there's no point in searching for answers to difficult questions?
   ● Is it saying that religious people think they have the right answers?
   ● Is it saying that it is important to keep asking the questions, even if you know there's probably not one 'right' answer?

THINK ABOUT IT!

3. Read through the questions from page 94, the questions posed by members of your class, and Hans Küng's ultimate questions. Work in pairs or small groups to organise the questions into different groups.

In this lesson you will:
- pose questions about meaning, purpose and truth
- explore and interpret some attempts to answer ultimate questions
- reflect on and express your own ideas about how far humans can really 'know' anything.

KEY WORDS

Mystic a person who tries to understand God by spending their life contemplating spiritual matters

Metaphor a way of understanding something by 'seeing' it as something else

THINK ABOUT IT!

1. What are you really sure about?
   - Is there any area where you feel you are an expert? Who would you describe as an expert? What do they know?
   - Are there some things you may never know? What things? Does this matter?

In the following poem, Alfred Lord Tennyson (1809–92) explored the question of how far humans can really understand whether there is a purpose behind the universe and, if so, what that purpose might be.

'Flower in the crannied wall,
I pluck you out of the crannies,
I hold you here, root and all, in my hand,
Little flower – if I could but understand
What you are, root and all, and all in all,
I should know what God and man is.'

Flower in the Crannied Wall by Alfred Lord Tennyson

● YOU WANT TO KNOW THE MEANING OF LIFE? JUST ASK THE COMPUTER!

In Douglas Adams' book *The Hitchhiker's Guide to the Galaxy* (1978) the characters ask their computer Deep Thought to tell them the answer to 'the meaning of life, the universe and everything'. It takes Deep Thought seven and a half million years to come up with an answer, but finally he tells them that the answer is forty two. The characters are not really satisfied with this but, as Deep Thought explains, they had not asked the right question in the first place!

In 2005 a group of German and British scientists programmed the biggest computer in Europe with known information about the universe and the laws of physics and asked it to compute a universe.

The Millennium Simulation will now be studied in detail, to try to answer all the questions that scientists have about the universe but have been unable to answer. For example, it is very difficult to ask any detailed questions of the real universe, but scientists can ask the simulation questions such as 'Where do black holes come from? How big are they? What do they do to galaxies?'

THINK ABOUT IT!

2. What other aspects of the natural world might inspire someone to write a poem exploring the meaning and purpose of life?

'We let it churn away ... and at the end we got this beautiful universe, which for all intents and purposes looks like the real thing.'

Professor C.S. Frenk, from the Institute of Computational Cosmology of Durham University

INFINITY? ETERNITY? HOLDING ON TO TIME

'To see the world in a grain of sand
And Heaven in a wild flower,
Hold Infinity in the palm of your hand
And Eternity in an hour.'

From 'Auguries of Innocence', a poem by William Blake (1757–1827)

JULIAN OF NORWICH

Julian of Norwich (c.1342–1416) was a Christian nun who lived as a recluse or hermit. She was also a **mystic** who experienced visions which she called 'showings'. In these showings she felt that God was communicating with her. Her writings show that many of her visions helped her to answer questions about the meaning of life. One of Julian's most well-known showings led her to see the meaning of life as a 'little thing' the size of a hazelnut.

'And he showed me a little thing the size of a hazelnut, on the palm of my hand, round like a ball. I looked at it thoughtfully and wondered, "What is this?" And the answer came, "It is all that is made." I marvelled that it continued to exist and did not suddenly disintegrate; it was so small. And again my mind supplied the answer, "It exists, both now and for ever, because God loves it." In short, everything owes its existence to the love of God.'

Revelations of Divine Love, chapter 5

THINK ABOUT IT!

3. **a)** What is William Blake saying in his poem that might answer the question 'What can we know'?
   b) What similarities can you see between Blake's poem and Tennyson's poem?
   c) Write your own four line poem starting, 'To see the world in...'

How did the Christian mystic Julian of Norwich see the world?

THINK ABOUT IT!

4. The **metaphor** in the two poems and in Julian's vision is about holding onto something to grasp its meaning and possess an ultimate truth. What would you hold on to, to symbolise 'all that is made'? Share and record your ideas.

In this lesson you will:
- explore and evaluate what really matters to people
- analyse the links between power and responsibility
- consider whether belief in God makes a difference to how people view the question of what really matters
- reflect on what matters to you and why.

THE END OF THE HUMAN RACE?

Some scientists have predicted that there is a possibility that humans may die out. The extract below was written by the naturalist and broadcaster David Attenborough, who is also a Humanist.

'There is no scientific evidence whatever to support the view and no reason to suppose that our stay on Earth will be any more permanent than that of the dinosaur. The processes of evolution are still going on among plants and birds, insects and mammals. So it is more than likely that if humans were to disappear from the face of the Earth, for whatever reason, there is a modest, unobtrusive creature somewhere that would develop into a new form and take our place.

'But although denying we have a special position in the natural world might seem becomingly modest in the eye of eternity, it might also be used as an excuse for evading our responsibilities. The fact is that no species has ever had such wholesale control over everything on Earth, living or dead, as we now have. That lays upon us, whether we like it or not, an awesome responsibility. In our hands now lies not only our own future, but that of all other living creatures with whom we share the Earth.'

THINK ABOUT IT!

1. Write on a sticky note what matters to you most in life. Stick your note onto a class sheet so that you can return to them at the end of the lesson.

How do David Attenborough's comments about humanity's place and role in the world make you feel?

THINK ABOUT IT!

2. 'If the human race dies out, does it matter?'
   a) Discuss this question in pairs.
   b) Share your ideas as a class and record the key points.

3. Does power bring responsibility? Do you agree with David Attenborough that because humanity has such power to control the Earth, we also have an 'awesome responsibility'? Discuss this answer as a class.

4. Might someone who believes in God agree or disagree with David Attenborough's view of humanity's place within the natural world? Give reasons for your answers.

A cartoon of a William Blake painting. What do you think the artist is saying?

THINK ABOUT IT!

5. Look at the two illustrations on this page. What messages are the two artists trying to get across?

6. Design your own cartoon or poster to make people think about whether they have responsibility for the future of life on Earth.

7. Vote with your thumb on the following: 'It doesn't matter if the human race dies out in the future.' – Agree / Disagree / Not sure?

8. Return to your sticky note from task 1, about what really matters to you. Is there anything you would add or change in light of your discussions in this lesson? Why?

What message do you think the artist, Luke Warm, is trying to convey through this poster?

In this lesson you will:
- explore some of the beliefs and experiences which have given people the courage to face challenges in their lives
- consider how faith impacts on some people's lives
- evaluate some beliefs about death
- reflect on what gives you courage to face the challenges in your life.

KEY WORDS

Envoy a messenger or representative who may be sent on a mission to help resolve conflict

Resurrection the belief that Jesus rose from the dead after his crucifixion. It can also mean a new life for Christians

CHRISTMAS IN CAPTIVITY

In 1987 Terry Waite, an **envoy** for the Church of England, was in Beirut to try and negotiate the release of Western hostages. However, he was captured himself and held hostage for nearly five years. For most of that time he was chained up, alone, in a cell with no natural light. After his release he wrote a book, *Taken On Trust*, about the 1763 days he spent as a hostage in Beirut.

> "Can you tell me the date, please?'"
> The familiar guard has been away for several days. His replacement is detached and appears somewhat surly. He replies curtly, "Twenty-four December."
> He snaps the padlock on my ankle and leaves the room. Tomorrow will be Christmas Day ... I wrap a blanket around my shoulders and read. The electricity is very inadequate now, and much of the time I read by the light of a candle. Next month I will have been a hostage for three years – the crucial 'make or break' period. It seems impossible. Three years since I had a normal conversation with anyone; three years since I saw the sun or felt the wind and the rain; three years in chains. How much longer can this go on? ... I plan my Christmas celebrations. Tonight I will celebrate the Holy Communion.
>
> From *Taken on Trust* by Terry Waite (1993)

THE COURAGE TO FACE DEATH

> "The most difficult and philosophically interesting question is how we should feel about death if it's the end."
>
> Thomas Nagel, Professor of Philosophy at New York University

THINK ABOUT IT!

1. What would you find the hardest thing to bear if you were held in captivity alone for years like Terry Waite and other hostages?

2. What do you think would give you the courage to keep going?

3. Prepare at least five questions you would like to ask Terry Waite about his captivity and faith. Some examples might be:

- What kept you going through this experience?
- How did you keep your faith alive?
- Did you ever doubt God?

Choose two of them and try to answer them as you think Terry would.

● A BUDDHIST PERSPECTIVE

Buddhists believe that when they die they will be reborn in another form, depending on how they have lived their former life. The Dalai Lama, the spiritual leader of the Tibetan people, was exiled from his home country of Tibet. Below he describes how he feels no fear of death, only concern at what will happen to his people.

> '"Sometimes when I think about death I get some kind of excitement. Instead of fear, I have a feeling of curiosity and this makes it easier for me to accept death. Of course, my only burden if I die today is, "Oh, what will happen to Tibet? What about Tibetan culture? What about six million Tibetan people's rights?" This is my main concern. Otherwise, I feel almost no fear of death.'
>
> *From* The Dalai Lama's Book of Wisdom *(1999)*.

● A CHRISTIAN PERSPECTIVE: BELIEF IN A RESURRECTION GIVES HOPE

Stanley Spencer often painted Christian subjects and events, but in the context of his own twentieth-century world. He included people he knew and loved, often in positions he had known them in when they were happy. In *The Resurrection at Cookham*, the dead are being resurrected in the churchyard in the village where Stanley Spencer lived. His wife is shown wearing one of her favourite sweaters. One girl is showing her dead friend the card on the wreath which she has put on her grave. The dead girl is thanking her friend for it. Stanley Spencer said that he had this idea when he saw a girl bringing a wreath to the grave of her dead friend and thought how wonderful it would be if her dead companion could read the card on the wreath and respond to it.

THINK ABOUT IT!

4. What do you think of Thomas Nagel's comment? Is it a terrible thing to go out of existence?

5. How could the prospect of death be exciting to the Dalai Lama?

THINK ABOUT IT!

6. Suppose a resurrection could happen in the way that Stanley Spencer painted it. How do you feel about this idea? What good things could come from it and what problems might occur?

◡ **'The Resurrection at Cookham' by Stanley Spencer (1891–1959).**

In this lesson you will:
- evaluate some religious and non-religious views about what humans should hold in contempt and what they should love and value
- reflect on what you would hold in contempt and what you love and value, and why.

KEY WORDS

Contempt to consider someone or something to be unworthy of respect

Arrogance to have an exaggerated sense of your own importance

Dogma a set of principles or ideas which are accepted as true without question

Ghetto a part of a city, often a slum area, where poor people live or are confined

In this lesson you will be looking at two accounts from people who both feel very strongly that some things human beings do to each other are unacceptable. Both writers are contemptuous of some human attitudes and actions. To show **contempt** means that you find something 'despicable' or unworthy of respect.

Jacob Bronowski was a Jewish Humanist scientist who wrote *The Ascent of Man* (1973).

'It is said that science will dehumanise people and turn them into numbers. This is false, tragically false. Look for yourself. This is the concentration camp and crematorium at Auschwitz. This, where people were turned into numbers. In that pond were flushed the ashes of some four million people. And that was not done by gas. It was done by **arrogance**. It was done by **dogma**. It was done by ignorance. When people believe that they have absolute knowledge, with no test in reality, this is how they behave. This is what men do when they aspire to the knowledge of gods.'

Jacob Bronowski, *The Ascent of Man (1973)*

● GREED IS GOODS

The following article is taken from the magazine for the homeless, *The Big Issue*. It was written by Martin Curtis, a homeless man living on the streets in the UK.

'The big high street shops are packed each Sunday. No church can get such numbers through its doors. Karl Marx said religion was the opium of the people. However, in post-millennium England, people worship the shops and absolve their sins by treating themselves to "a little something".

'"Retail therapy" it's called. In Africa people starve, and in England people buy Gucci jewellery so they don't feel so bad about living in this world of extremes. In this country starvation and gluttony exist, doors from one another. But instead of giving a poor person a sandwich, most people do a spot of retail therapy.

'Next Sunday, I'll go back to the **ghetto** and starve. Retail therapy is greed by any other name. Think about it and keep flaunting those labels, eh?'

Greed is goods by Martin Curtis, *May 2005*

THINK ABOUT IT!

1. **a)** Are you sometimes convinced that you are absolutely 'right'? Discuss with a partner an occasion when you have felt like this.

   b) Find some other examples (historical or current) where people have treated others badly because they were convinced that they were 'right'.

   c) What part was played by 'arrogance', 'dogma' and 'ignorance' in your examples?

THINK ABOUT IT!

2. Martin Curtis has posed his own 'Think about it' question. What has his article made you think about?

3. Do you agree with Curtis that 'Retail therapy is greed by any other name'? Give reasons for your answer.

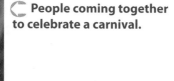

People coming together to celebrate a carnival.

Wallets of the victims of the holocaust during World War II.

Over one million Cambodians were killed by the Khmer Rouge between 1975 and 1979.

What will give this newborn baby the courage to face whatever life throws at her?

THINK ABOUT IT!

Look carefully at the pictures on this page.

4. a) Working in groups, half the class will create a concept map on 'Contempt' and the other half will create a concept map on 'Love'. You should use both words and images for the concept maps.

Look for relevant pictures and information in newspapers and magazines, and on the Internet. For recommended websites go to www.heinemann.co.uk/hotlinks and enter the express code 7355P, then click on the relevant section.

b) When you have finished, display the maps and walk round looking at each other's work. Ask questions about why people have chosen their images and text.

In this lesson you will:
- explore how religious and other sources impact on people's decisions on how to act
- explain how reasons can be used in different ways to provide answers to ethical questions and dilemmas
- reflect on what influences your own decisions and views regarding how people should act.

KEY WORDS

Dilemma a situation where a difficult choice has to be made between two alternatives

Moral dilemma a situation where a difficult choice has to be made about whether something is right or wrong

Innocent pure, free from moral wrong

Utilitarianism a theory based on the assumption that what is 'good' is whatever brings the most happiness to the greatest number of people

● NO CHOICE BUT TO CHOOSE

Think of a time when you faced a really difficult choice between two decisions or courses of action. Perhaps neither was what you really wanted to do but you had to choose. Perhaps you made a choice but felt that you *ought* to have done something else. Such a situation is referred to as a '**dilemma**'. If the decision you faced involved choices about right and wrong, then it was a **moral dilemma**.

THINK ABOUT IT!

1. What makes an action right or wrong?

2. 'Are right and wrong the same for everyone?' Discuss this question in pairs then share your views as a class.

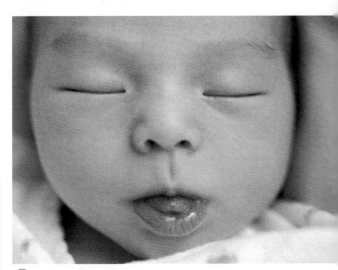

🎧 Is a newborn baby innocent?

In Book 2 you considered Edmund Burke's statement that 'for evil to triumph it is only necessary for good men to do nothing.' This idea, that to choose *not* to act makes someone just as guilty as if they had done something bad, is at the heart of a speech given by the Christian Pastor, Martin Niemoller (1892–1984).

Niemoller was a German Lutheran who fought as an ace submarine commander in the First World War (1914–18). He offered to serve in the German navy in the Second World War (1939–45), despite his outspoken opposition to Hitler. In retaliation for preaching against Hitler and the Nazi Party, Niemoller's house was ransacked by the Gestapo and he was imprisoned for seven years in the concentration camps at Sachsenhausen and Dachau.

'First they came for the Jews
And I did not speak out because I was not a Jew.
Then they came for the communists
And I did not speak out because I was not a communist.
Then they came for the trade unionists
And I did not speak out because I was not a trade unionist.
Then they came for me
And there was no one left to speak out for me.'

From a speech written by Martin Niemoller in 1946.

● HOW GOOD WAS THE GOOD SAMARITAN?

You have probably heard the story of the Good Samaritan many times before. It is one of the most famous parables told by Jesus. Jesus told it in response to a question from a learned lawyer who wanted to know *exactly* how to interpret a teaching in the law.

> 'On one occasion an expert in the law stood up to test Jesus. "Teacher," he asked, "what must I do to inherit eternal life?"
>
> "What is written in the Law?" Jesus replied. "How do you read it?"
>
> He answered: "'Love the Lord your God with all your heart and with all your soul and with all your strength and with all your mind'; and 'Love your neighbour as yourself.'"
>
> "You have answered correctly," Jesus replied. "Do this and you will live."
>
> But he wanted to justify himself, so he asked Jesus, "And who is my neighbour?"
>
> In reply Jesus said: "A man was going down from Jerusalem to Jericho, when he fell into the hands of robbers. They stripped him of his clothes, beat him and went away, leaving him half-dead. A priest happened to be going down the same road and, when he saw the man, he passed by on the other side. So too, a Levite, when he came to the place and saw him, passed by on the other side. But a Samaritan, as he travelled, came where the man was; and when he saw him, he took pity on him. He went to him and bandaged his wounds, pouring on oil and wine. Then he put the man on his own donkey, brought him to an inn and took care of him. The next day he took out two silver coins and gave them to the innkeeper. 'Look after him,' he said, 'and when I return, I will reimburse you for any extra expense you may have.'
>
> "Which of these three do you think was a neighbour to the man who fell into the hands of robbers?"
>
> The expert in the law replied, "The one who had mercy on him."
>
> Jesus told him, "Go and do likewise."'
>
> *The Bible, Luke 10: 25–37*

THINK ABOUT IT!

3. Why do you think Christians believe this parable is so important? Compare your ideas with a partner.

4. What are the most important influences in your life that help you to decide how to behave, how to treat others, what you should value and what not to say or do? How do you know what guidance to choose? How can you test it?

5. Return to question 2. Have you changed your position at all?

● UTILITARIANISM – THE GREATEST HAPPINESS FOR THE GREATEST NUMBER?

In the nineteenth century the philosophers Jeremy Bentham (1748–1832) and John Stuart Mill (1806–73) developed an idea known as '**utilitarianism**'. This was based on the belief that living in a way that ensured your actions were, as far as possible, those that produced the most pleasure and the least pain would ensure 'the greatest happiness for the greatest number'.

🎧 **The road from Jerusalem to Jericho was a lonely and dangerous place for travellers.**

In this lesson you will:
- understand the meaning of hope
- examine some of the beliefs which have inspired people to work for a better future
- explore the idea of 'vision' and what inspires people to hope
- reflect on your own vision and hopes for yourself and for the future of the world.

KEY WORDS

Visionary someone who plans for the future with wisdom, imagination and originality

Justice the principle that everyone has the right to be treated fairly

Conflict resolution helping to solve problems peacefully

THE STORY OF PANDORA'S BOX

In this Greek legend the world was a perfect place where there was no anger, or hatred, no hunger or disease, no laziness or cruelty. It was so perfect that the gods themselves were jealous and decided to punish humans by introducing all kinds of trouble.

The great god Zeus created a young woman, Pandora, and sent her to Earth, giving her a mysterious box to take with her. On Earth she met, fell in love with and married a young man, Epimetheus. He warned Pandora that she must never open the box in case it brought trouble, but Pandora was curious about the box. She looked at it closely and thought that she heard strange whispering sounds coming from inside. Surely, she thought, one little peep could do no harm?

Pandora slowly lifted the lid. Immediately, out flew the ugliest creatures she had ever seen. She tried to close the lid, but it was too late. The creatures were the Spites that cause trouble on Earth – Hatred, Cruelty, Anger, Greed, Fear, Jealousy, Old Age and Disease. Pandora could not stop them as they flew to every part of the world.

When the box was empty, Pandora shut the lid. Suddenly she heard a soft tapping and a voice whispering 'Let me out, let me out'. She opened the lid and out flew the last thing left in the box. It was a bird-like creature with beautiful, shining wings. It was Hope. Hope also flew to the far corners of the Earth, so wherever there are troubles there is also Hope.

WANTED! 'VISIONARIES FOR A JUST AND PEACEFUL WORLD'.

The Joseph Rowntree Charitable Trust is a charity which uses interest from money left by the **Quaker** multi-millionaire Joseph Rowntree (1836–1925) to undertake research into social difficulties and how to improve them. Rowntree believed that determined individuals can change the world for the better, so in 2004 the Trust set up a competition to allow seven **visionaries** the opportunity to achieve their dreams for a better world. The applicants had to summarize their dreams in 100 words and were judged against criteria that the projects should be based on **justice**, equality, peace, and **conflict resolution**.

THINK ABOUT IT!

1. This story of Pandora's Box is a myth or a legend. Do you think it contains any truths? Summarize the story using no more than three key points.

2. What hopes do you have for yourself?

3. What hopes do you have for the world?

4. The Russian writer Dostoyevsky said: 'To live without hope is to cease to live.' In pairs, discuss what you think he meant by this and whether you agree with him.

THINK ABOUT IT!

5. Organize a class competition to find a visionary.

    a) Each pupil must present their own application for a project to create a more just and peaceful world in just 100 words. You might like to revisit some of the inspirational people you have studied in your RE lessons to help with your vision. For example:

    - *Martin Luther King:* 'I have a dream...'
    - *Gandhi:* 'Non-violence is not a garment to be put on and off at will. Its seat is in the heart, and it must be an inseparable part of our very being.'
    - *Gandhi:* 'I claim to be no more than the average person with less than average ability. I have not the shadow of a doubt that any man or woman can achieve what I have, if he or she would make the same effort and cultivate the same hope and faith.'
    - *The Bible, Isaiah 2: 4:* The prophet Isaiah wrote that at the Last Judgement people would 'beat their swords into ploughs and their spears into pruning hooks: nation shall not lift up sword against nation, neither shall they learn war anymore.'

    b) Appoint a panel of judges to evaluate the entries against Joseph Rowntree's criteria and present a prize to the seven most visionary proposals. You could ask older students, teachers, parents and governors to be on the panel.

● **THE TREE OF LIFE**

The Mozambique **civil war** (1976–93) tore the nation apart and caused widespread economic misery and famine. After the war ended the local Anglican Bishop, Dom Dinis Sengulane, set up a scheme called Transforming Arms into Tools. This rewarded communities who handed in their weapons by giving them useful machinery such as sewing machines and tractors. So that everyone could see that the weapons could never be used again, Sengulane asked sculptors to transform them into public works of art.

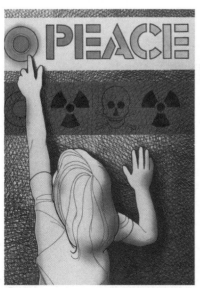

THINK ABOUT IT!

6. Are there ever situations when it is pointless to hope?

This inscription by an unknown victim was found on the wall of a concentration camp cell in Nazi Germany:
'I believe in the sun even when it is not shining.
I believe in love where feeling is not.
I believe in God even if He is silent.'

⌒ This sculpture was made by Kester Hilario Nhatugueja, Fiel dos Santos and Adelino Serafim Mate in Mozambique in 2004. The tree is three metres high and made from weapons (all of them made in Europe) that killed and maimed thousands of people in the Mozambique civil war. It shows not only the tree but the insects and animals that live in and around it.

⌒ **Write a caption or title for this picture. Share your ideas as a class and vote for the best one.**

WHAT THIS TASK IS ALL ABOUT:

Complete either question 1 or question 2.

1. Work in small groups to prepare an assembly for Year 9 on the theme 'Are there more questions than answers?'

   - Write Hans Kung's questions in your own words and use them as a starting point for a sequence of words and images (use PowerPoint or a similar presentation package) to help people reflect on the questions. You can add background music if you like.
   - Use information from the book and what you have collected from newspapers, magazines and other sources. If you have the technology available, you can include relevant video or DVD extracts.
   - Present your assembly to the class. You may decide to choose one assembly or combine your ideas to create an assembly that your class leads for the whole of Year 9.

2. Individually, choose two of Hans Kung's questions and write them in your own words. Then, create a PowerPoint presentation or poster to illustrate the questions, using words and images to show some of the different ways in which people might answer them. Present your work to the class.

WHAT YOU NEED TO DO TO COMPLETE THE TASK:

You should write a short summary of your poster, presentation or assembly, explaining how you or your group developed ideas, what the key ideas were, and why the words, images and music were chosen.

HINTS AND TIPS

- You must be able to justify your choice of words and images, showing how they are relevant to the topic.
- If you are working as a group, it is important that you keep a note of:
  - how you work together
  - how you generate and share your ideas
  - who was responsible for different aspects of the activity.

TO ACHIEVE	YOU WILL NEED TO
Level 4	Use some religious vocabulary to describe beliefs, ideas, feelings and experiences and how they affect people's lives. Show that you can ask questions of meaning and purpose and suggest some answers to them from different perspectives. Explain where you look for inspiration in your own life.
Level 5	Ask questions and suggest answers, relating them to your own and other people's experiences. Show that you understand that people have different ways of answering ultimate questions. Analyse what influences and inspires you in the search for meaning and purpose in your life.
Level 6	Use religious and philosophical language to describe the beliefs and ideas in your assembly/presentation. Show that you can interpret the visual and written examples you have chosen, explaining how they might be used to answer ultimate questions by people from different traditions and belief backgrounds. Show you understand your own and other people's views on questions of identity, belonging, meaning, purpose and truth.
Level 7	Use a wide range of religious and philosophical vocabulary. Show that you can analyse the issues and values that lie behind the questions of meaning and truth which you have explored. Use a wide range of sources and forms of expression in your assembly/presentation. Show that you can make a critical, personal response to the issues which lie behind the ultimate questions you have explored.

GLOSSARY

Abortion premature removal of the baby from the womb during pregnancy

Agape Christian concept of unconditional love

Ahimsa non-violence, respect for life

Akirah Islamic belief in life after death

Anglican Church the body of churches around the world that are in communion with the Church of England

Animal experimentation to perform scientific research using animals

Apostles disciples 'sent out' by Jesus

Argument from design an argument suggesting the universe is designed and therefore requires a designer, God

Arrogance to have an exaggerated sense of your own importance

Bhagavard Gita a sacred Hindu text of a dialogue between the god Krishna and Prince Arujna on the eve of a great battle

Big Bang a huge explosion that many scientists believe started the universe

Big Crunch theory that the universe will one day collapse back in on itself

Blood transfusion replacement of lost blood by donor blood

Chastity not having sex until you are married

Cloning inserting an adult's genetic information into an egg cell to produce an offspring which is genetically identical to its parent

Collaboration working together to achieve a common goal

Community of enquiry allowing pupils to work as a group, focusing on a story or quote to generate their own questions and to explore them in depth

Conflict resolution helping to solve problems peacefully

Conscience a person's sense of right and wrong

Contempt to consider something or someone to be unworthy of respect

Conversion process of changing from one belief to another

Creation the belief that the Earth and the universe was deliberately created by God or gods or some divine force

Creation Science the attempt to show that science supports the idea of creation

Culture a way of life based on the customs of a particular time or place

Denomination different branches of the Christian Church

Design a pattern, suggesting arrangement

Dialogue communication, discussion of different viewpoints

Dilemma a situation where a difficult choice has to be made between two alternatives

Divine revelation the special revelation of God to believers

DNA deoxyribonucleic acid: the building block of cell life

Dogma a set of principles or ideas which are accepted as true without question

Dominion control over, or responsibility for, the Earth

Dowry an amount of money which has to be paid to the family of a woman's husband when she gets married

Embryo unborn offspring

Enlightenment the process of becoming aware of the truth of existence which frees a person to obtain Nirvana

Envoy a messenger or representative who may be sent on a mission to help resolve conflict

Eternity time without beginning or end, forever

Euthanasia helping someone to painlessly end their own life

Evolution development of species from earlier forms

Fatwa guidance for Muslims based on the Qu'ran

Gender being male or female

General revelation God or the divine, experienced by creation or conscience

Genetic inherited characteristics in animals and plants

Genetic engineering manipulation of genetic material

Genetic inheritance the genes humans receive from their parents

Ghetto a part of a city, often a slum area, where poor people live or are confined

Global ethic a code of conduct for the whole world

Haiku a type of poem devised by Zen Buddhists

Hijab a head covering used by Muslim women

Holocaust a term used to describe large-scale destruction, used in connection with the persecution of the Jews and other groups by the Nazis in the 1930s and 1940s

Hope the desire and search for a future good

Humanist someone who believes that all values should be based on human experience and reason

Infertile state of being unable to conceive offspring

Infinity something that has no end or limits

Injustice unfairness

Innocence pure, free from moral wrong

Intelligent design the belief that there is scientific evidence to support the Genesis story of a creator God

Inter-faith dialogue discussions and work carried out between different faiths

In-Vitro Fertilisation (IVF) process of fertilising an egg in a test tube before replacing it in the womb

Justice the principle that everyone has the right to be treated fairly

Karma a teaching which states that all actions have consequences and will influence future lives

Koans paradoxical questions used by Zen Buddhists to discover truth

Levite follower of a religious group from the time of Jesus who did not believe in resurrection

Meditation calming and strengthening the mind by concentrating

Metanarrative a " big story", such as a religion or a political belief, that helps shape a person's life

Metaphor a way of understanding something by 'seeing' it as something else

Mishnah a special, ancient book of Jewish teachings and thoughts

Modernism a philosophy based on reason and science

Moral dilemma a situation where a difficult choice has to be made about whether something is right or wrong

Mystic a person who tries to understand God by spending their life in contemplation of spiritual matters

Natural selection 'survival of the fittest', the theory at the heart of evolution

Nihilism the belief that existence has no point

Nirvana state of being free from confusion, greed or hatred

Non-conformist Christian denominations which broke away from the Church of England

Ordained having a special service to become a priest or minister

Pagan a belief in many gods and that nature should be worshipped

Parable a story told to illustrate a religious or moral idea

Philosopher someone who thinks deeply and asks questions to try and understand the meaning of life

Post-modernism a group of ideas that question whether there is an objective truth

Prejudice believing some people are inferior or superior without even knowing them

Pro-Choice the viewpoint that it is the mother's right to decide whether or not to have an abortion

Pro-Life the viewpoint that it is the baby's right to live and that abortion is morally wrong

Quakers Christian group, otherwise known as the Religious Society of Friends, which was established by George Fox in the 17th century and which advocates pacifism

Rapture, the the belief, held by some Christians, that they will leave Earth to go to heaven before the Second Coming

Recluse a person who withdraws from the world to live alone, in isolation

Reconciliation putting aside past troubles

Reincarnation the belief that after death a person's soul moves into another body and continues to live

Respect to feel or show admiration for something or someone you believe has good qualities

Resurrection the belief that Jesus rose from the dead after his crucifixion. It can also mean a new life for Christians

Revelation God making himself known to people

Reversion Muslim belief that all are born Muslim and wander away from this faith, but then return to their first belief

Sacred something of God or the divine

Samaritan a person who voluntarily offers help in times of trouble

Sanctity purity or holiness

Sanctity of life the idea that all life comes from God and is therefore holy

Science study of the physical, biological and chemical processes of the universe

Second Coming the Christian belief that Jesus will return at the end of time

Secular a non-religious way of life or thinking

Sex sexual intercourse

Socratic dialogue asking questions in order to discover truth

Special Revelation the belief that God, or the divine, reveals to believers in particular ways

Stereotype a fixed, unchanged idea about a person or group of people, usually based on prejudice

Stewardship human responsibility to look after the world and everything in it; looking after something so it can be passed on to the next generation

Suicide the act of deliberately ending your own life

Theologian someone who thinks about questions raised by and about religions

Transplant transfer of an organ or tissue from one being to another

Trimurti the three gods of creation, sustaining, and destruction – Brahma, Vishnu and Shiva

Turin Shroud a piece of cloth that Jesus' body was supposed to have been wrapped in after the crucifixion

Ultimate questions questions about the meaning and purpose of life, death and the place of humans in the universe

Utilitarianism a theory based on the assumption that what is 'good' is whatever brings the most happiness to the greatest number of people

Visionary someone who plans for the future with wisdom, imagination and originality

Xenotransplantation transplant of animal organs to humans

Zen Buddhism a type of Buddhism developed in China and Japan

INDEX